ELEGY FOR A BROKEN SOLDIER

A UN MISSION THAT CHANGED A YOUNG SOLDIER'S LIFE FOREVER

CHRIS McQUAID

Strategic Book Publishing and Rights Co.

Strategic Book Publishing and Rights Co., LLC
USA | Singapore
www.sbpra.com

For information about special discounts for bulk purchases, please contact Strategic Book Publishing and Rights Co., LLC Special Sales, at bookorder@sbpra.net.

ISBN: 978-1-949483-99-4

To the memory of our neighbour and family friend, Trooper Anthony Browne, BMC, a brave young soldier who died tragically at Niemba, Congo in November 1960 while serving with the Irish Defence Forces and the United Nations in the cause of peace.

CONTENTS

FOREWORD

The compelling story Chris McQuaid tells in his memoir is as much a story about the evolution of modern Ireland as it is about his own experiences progressing through the ranks of the Defence Forces.

On one hand this book is as much a social history of Ireland and its armed forces as it is a personal history. The early days of McQuaid's life are recent enough for many readers to relate to from their own memory of that era. However, they also act as a valuable record for the more youthful generations reading.

McQuaid's tale is an important one. Many readers in Ireland know very little about their military and how it is structured and maintained. This is particularly apparent in the lack of understanding in civilian Ireland of the social configuration of our Defence Forces. There is a class structure in Ireland - subtle as it sometimes is, but very real nevertheless, and there is certainly a social hierarchy in the Defence Forces.

While Rank and hierarchy are essential elements to run any disciplined force that is given the responsibility of exercising lethal force on behalf of the State, the Irish Defence Force now luxuriates in the glow of the most up-to-date workplace legislation. This legislation protects its members from abuse of power and bullying. It also still allows the organisation the necessary leeway to prepare new entrants for the physical and psychological rigours that active service will bring.

However, it was not always so and seeing life in the forces through McQuaid's all-seeing eye brings the reader on a singular social, historical and military journey.

You see McQuaid is part of a unique bunch of soldiers from his generation. He managed to make the gargantuan leap from the enlisted ranks to the commissioned officer ranks – no mean achievement for any soldier to achieve in what was then a deeply conservative institution residing in a very inward looking and reactionary society.

For any interested student of social affairs that alone makes the book worth reading. McQuaid's perceptions and ability to adjust to his new position are remarkable given how he would have been conditioned very differently at the beginning of his career.

As if this was not enough was the fact that when he received his commission as a newly minted officer, McQuaid was already well on his way to earning a Bachelor of Commerce degree on his own time. Climbing the ranks and advancing into third level education were major milestones for a man who had commenced life in respectable but financially humble circumstances in the little working-class Dublin suburb of Rialto.

However, the really eye-opening and most important aspect of Captain Chris McQuaid's story is the trauma he was to suffer very early on in his military career.

Undoubtedly this trauma was to affect Chris for the rest of his career, indeed the rest of his life. The fact that he managed to advance in his career and education with the spectre of this trauma dogging his every step is testimony to the man's dogged nature and the strong character forged by his parents and their Rialto upbringing.

While harrowing to read and as hard-hitting as a hammer blow between the eyes, there is a positive aspect to reading the of Chris's trauma. For the reader the early shock that will assail them is soon replaced by anger at how the young soldier that was then Private Chris McQuaid was treated by those who should have looked out for him.

But despite the shock, the anger and a variety of other attendant emotions the reader will experience as they see these episodes through the eyes of Chris McQuaid, they will ultimately be uplifted. Uplifted by the strength of the human spirit displayed, the reader will be struck by the additional sense of resilience also displayed as Chris gets back up from each slap down he receives.

Make no mistake, this book is no fairy-tale. While he overcame much, there were many things resulting from his trauma that went on to blight Chris's life – indeed still do.

But there is a message of hope that is redolent throughout. This message can be summed up in one word: resilience! Chris, despite it all, continues to exhibit resilience. He has suffered, physically and more importantly psychologically. He bears the scars of his battles nobly – and he continues to look to his front and march on.

At a time when mental health issues are no longer taboo, and we are comfortable talking about matters that have traumatised our society and our youth, we still struggle with building resilience. Yes, we have re-built and re-ignited our values of tolerance, forgiveness and hope. But we still grapple with developing the necessary tools of resilience.

Now more than ever, Chris McQuaid's lessons in applied resilience in the face of extreme adversity are a beacon for those in our society who are at risk of being overwhelmed by despair, dislocation and indeed suicidal ideation.

McQuaid's story may hark back to an Ireland past, but its relevance, now more than ever, is bang up-to-date for the Ireland of today.

Declan Power,
Dublin
May 2017

PREFACE

This snapshot of events in my life, begun in 2013 was a painful and disturbing journey back in time. I did not set out to create a work of literature. I did not sketch out each paragraph or chapter, to begin with. I wrote while standing at my laptop, placed on my piano. I began to write because I wanted to vent my anger. I wanted to rail at injustice and I wanted to expose the perpetrators. The result was a 'stream of consciousness', frantic and unforgiving, triggered by the effects of anaesthetic drugs. What I was really doing was giving some sort of shape to persistent thoughts of revenge and to feelings that were often overwhelming and un-nameable. Vindictive and cruel words were vomited out, my rage masked by what I would slowly and painfully come to realise were feelings of need, hurt and helplessness.

If I had known then where it would lead I might have given up and indeed, on at least two occasions during the subsequent writing process, I almost did. I have learned much in the process, and if there is one message to be taken from the book, it is this: never give up!

Chris McQuaid, Dublin, 2018

CHAPTER 1

An Innocent Is Born

When somewhere, from deep within me, there arises
the vivid sense of having been a child,
the purity and essence of that childhood
where I once lived: then I can't bear to know it.
I want to form an angel from that sense
and hurl him upwards, into the front row
of angels who cry out, remembering God.

Requiem for a Friend, Rainer Maria Rilke

Most Irish people born during the latter half of the 20th century remember the country in black and white, or in varying shades of grey. Church and State figures clad in dark suits or black robes oversaw every aspect of our lives. From as far back as the 1800s the religious orders controlled the education systems and the main purpose of their schools was to implant religious ideals and values into their students. The education system was viewed by the State as an ideological device rather than a place for young people to gain knowledge and achieve a qualification. John Coolahan, described in an *Irish Times* article in October, 2009 as 'the man who knows more than anyone about Irish education', said that the Irish government in the 1950s had prioritised the promotion of 'true Irish' or 'Gaelic cultural heritage' through the school curricula and demonstrated far less interest in the 'social aspects of educational provision'. 'English trash', in the form of newsprint, periodicals and radio was to be avoided.

"Burn everything British except their coal," my father's aunt

Bridget used to say. Hers was the mind-set of a people on the cusp of freedom from eight hundred years of British domination. She, like many of her contemporaries, dressed in black. Grand-aunt Bridget was actually a very refined woman, a Cavan woman, former housekeeper to a canon, first in Malahide, an affluent district in north Dublin and later in the village of Enniskerry in County Wicklow. Living and working in such an environment, it is likely that she was anti-Protestant rather than anti-British and like most people in Ireland she was happy enough to buy and wear and consume goods, many of which originated in the United Kingdom. Like my mother, she liked music and the 'finer things in life' and she was especially kind and generous. The kitchen in the cannon's house was below stairs and led out into a cultivated garden. Bridget cooked and baked on a gigantic black range that gave off tremendous heat. I loved visiting her and sitting in the warm and cosy kitchen, made all the more welcoming by Bridget's home baking and home-made jam. Canon Kennedy, for whom she worked was a friend of the family and as a boy, my father often fished with him. Fr. John Sullivan was a regular visitor to the canon's house. He was known as a healer and a very compassionate man and when he died his remains were brought to St Francis Xavier's church in Gardiner Street. It is now a place where people come to pray and bring their petitions to Fr. John, asking him to intercede for them with his prayers. When grand-aunt Bridget died, her coffin was placed beside his coffin at his shrine, on the eve of her burial. Fr. Sullivan was beatified on May 13th, 2017. Someday I may be one hand-shake away from a saint!

I was born the second of seven children in Dublin's national maternity hospital in 1945 and grew up in Rialto at a time when the mass indoctrination of previous decades was slowly being eroded. Outside influences slowly penetrated the Irish psyche. Because of the Cold War, American troops maintained a presence in many European countries and their influence spread across much of the continent, mainland Britain and eventually to the general public in Ireland. 'Westerns' or to us, 'Cowboy films' began appearing in local cinemas. Foreign games had also taken hold. My father was an ardent soccer fan who had played as centre forward at inter-club level with a club in Bray. His 'away team' idols were Manchester United. His home team was Shamrock Rovers and as a child, I rode on the crossbar of his bicycle, with my head tucked beneath his chin to watch the team play at Milltown.

My father began his working life as a solicitor's clerk in Enniskerry, in Wicklow, then worked for Monument Creameries, delivering milk throughout the city. When the Monument Creamery closed my father found work at a bakery. He then worked at the National Museum. Hard working, a strong disciplinarian and a believer in justice, he had no hesitation in delivering corporal punishment whenever we strayed from the hard and fast household rules. Nor did he hesitate to act in the event of an emergency. In December 1954 he plunged into the freezing waters of the Grand Canal near our home in Rialto to rescue a man from drowning. A member of An Gárda Síochána called to the house to inform my mother of the incident, and although my father had the good sense to remove his shoes and pants before diving into the Canal Basin, he had been taken to hospital suffering from mild hypothermia. He was awarded the Certificate of Bravery by the State in August 1956.

My first experience of injustice was in St. James' Boys School, run by Irish Christian Brothers where religious ideals and values ranked supreme. Someone had spat on a holy picture, a plastic-coated card with a picture of the Virgin Mary on the front and a prayer on the back. The teacher asked for the culprit to own up. No-one moved, whereupon he called everyone to the front of the class, ordered each one of us to hold out our hand and doled out a severe beating with a cane. Not all Brothers taught by the rule of the cane, however. One younger Brother who took choir class had a liking for opera and taught us 'The Huntsman's Chorus', from *Der*

Freischütz by Carl Maria von Weber. It was a change from 'O'Donnell Abú' and the Gregorian chant of the Latin Mass.

Like most Catholic families of the time, ours observed Sunday Mass, Mass on holy days of obligation, Lenten ceremonies, religious processions, regular confession and attendance at the church during vigils and novenas. Having started school with the nuns in Basin Lane, I had a good grounding in Catechism, prayers and hymns, cajoled by Sister Imelda who was warm, gentle and always smiling. Every night at home, kitchen chairs were pulled out and we knelt with our elbows propped on them, beads in hand, for the Rosary; my father, whose faith was as fervent as his discipline, knelt with his back to us, leading the prayer. Although united in faith, my parents were divided in many other ways and they seemed to argue a lot. To escape from arguments, my father would take himself off to his greenhouse at the bottom of the garden where he grew tomatoes, lettuce and a variety of other vegetables. He loved food and sport. My mother loved classical music.

My eldest brother was thirteen, the one behind me was ten and my sister was aged eight and none of us knew anything about babies until the arrival of three more. My only knowledge of babies had come from a religious context and my time in Junior and Senior Infants in Basin Lane. Christmas was the birthday of Baby, Jesus whose mother was Mary, Our Lady. Each year in May, during 'Our Lady's Feast Day' there was a very large procession in which all children from the convent and all boys, big and small, from the Christian Brothers' School across the road took part, singing hymns as we followed the priest and acolytes through the streets. One hymn that I still remember more than all others is, 'I'll Sing a Hymn to Mary'. We knew the words by heart:

I'll sing a hymn to Mary, the mother of my God,
The virgin of all virgins of David's royal blood,
Oh! teach me, Holy Mary, a loving song to frame,

When wicked men blaspheme thee,
I'll love and bless thy name.
Oh! Lily of the Valley, Oh mystic Rose,
What tree or flower, e'en the fairest, is half so fair as thee?

They meant absolutely nothing. I hadn't a clue what 'virgin' was, let alone 'mystic'. What occupied our young minds was the tea and scones which awaited us when the procession was over. I remember asking my mother, "Mammy, what does mystic rose mean?" Mother was busy making an apple dumpling, boiling it in a linen cloth in a large pot of boiling water. Served with custard, it was delicious, a rare treat. "Wait for your father to come home," she said. I must have known instinctively not to ask what virgin meant. When my father came home I was too busy eating to remember to ask him about mystic and virgin.

I have only one memory of my mother being in hospital. It was when my youngest brother was born. The news of his impending arrival home was not exactly welcomed by the six established residents, all vying for food, space and attention. Serious negotiations took place between two significant matriarchs who carried some influence in the family, one my grandaunt, Bridget, the other my fathers' sister who was also my godmother. In the end, there was no question of "Baby" not being brought home. It would be a quiet baby, we were told, so we agreed. He was a very good baby and we loved him. We had so much fun with him when he was learning to walk, and I developed a special bond with him.

I graduated to a technical school in Chapel Street. On my first day the metalwork teacher introduced himself to the class and then proceeded to draw a semi-circle around where he was standing and warned us not to venture beyond it. "All boys are smelly," he declared. How could I be one of those? I wondered. My mother washed us to within an inch of our lives every Saturday. My father checked or necks for 'watermarks' every day and with our heads in a grip like a vice, he fine-combed our hair, examining our scalps for head lice.

I was fifteen when I ran away from home. An older school friend had extended family in Liverpool and he told me that he was going there to find work. It sounded like an adventure, a trip by boat across the Irish Sea and a big city that maybe held more excitement and more to do than whizzing on my bicycle down Watling Hill and around the roads in Rialto. I sold my bicycle and bought a boat ticket and off we went. His parents knew he was going but my parents were ignorant of my plans. My friend's parents knew that I was going too but they didn't say anything to my parents. I simply left without a word. On arrival in Liverpool Docks, the full realisation of what I had done hit me. I was sick with guilt and rooted to the spot on the quay. "Aren't you coming?" my friend asked. "No," I said. "What are you going to do?" he asked. "I'm going home." I had enough money for a return ticket and a packet of crisps to sustain me for the boat journey back to Dublin. When I returned home, it was as if nothing had happened. Not one word was said, and life carried on as normal.

A year later, education over, I found part-time work in a high-quality restaurant in O'Connell Street. Bob, the baker used to bake soda bread in the old ovens behind the restaurant. I'd take some of his morning mix and do my own baking, much to the amusement of my nanny and aunt. My soda bread offerings were rock hard. Bob finally told my father and my baking career came to an abrupt end. I then got a job as a copy-boy with *The Irish Times*. It was during the Shanahan Stamp case, the financial scandal which erupted around Shanahan's Stamp Auctions in 1959. The scam was orchestrated by Paul Singer, a con man who is said to have played on the greed of unsophisticated investors, desperate to make a few pounds during the gloom of 1950s Ireland. When the story broke, journalists were pinned to their desks, their phones and their typewriters and I was kept on my toes, running errands for them. Trips to the offices of *The Cork Examiner* yielded five shillings. In between errands I made tea for the journalists and got them ginger nut biscuits from the basement canteen. I eventually got a job in the art department at Cassidy's Department Store in George's Street. Cassidy's employed an English display artist who mounted displays of a very high standard in the windows. I wheeled a handcart with display craft and materials from Thomas Street to Georges Street for a fashion show organised by the store in the Mansion House, no expense spared. We worked all through the night before the event, which was an outstanding success. At weekends I worked in a bicycle shop. I declined the offer of an apprenticeship at the bicycle shop, fixing punctured tyres and assembling new cycles. The offer included training at the Raleigh bicycle manufacturers in Nottingham, England to learn how to spoke wheels. Although a craft in itself, it seemed tedious and repetitive. My clandestine visit to Liverpool must have indicated a yearning for adventure but instead of sneaking off again, I needed an orderly transition into the world of work.

Changes had been afoot in the echelons of power for almost a decade. Free secondary school education, introduced in 1966, would come too late for me but two significant factors contributed to the shift from the inward-looking Church and State policies of the 1940s and '50s to the establishment of our country's role on the world stage. One was Ireland's admission to the United Nations and the other, the initiation of a programme for economic recovery. In 1951 I had just started school at Basin Lane in Dublin when Seán Lemass, veteran of the 1916 Easter Rising and the War of Independence, became Minister for Industry and Commerce. Lemass believed that a new economic policy was needed. But in the government mansion on Kildare Street T.K. (Ken) Whitaker, a thirty-five-year-old public servant from Rostrevor, north of the border was writing up a paper entitled, 'Economic Development' out of which grew the Programme for Economic Expansion. The programme gave new hope to a country with a stagnant economy and mounting unemployment. Whitaker's programme was embraced by Seán Lemass and when Lemass became Taoiseach, tax breaks and grants were provided by his government to foreign firms wishing to set up operations in Ireland. Between them, Seán Lemass and TK Whitaker launched an integrated system of national development and the framework of the modern Irish economy.

Ireland's active participation at the United Nations would have an enormous impact on global issues. At home, its effects would run deep. Thousands of Irish families would offer sons, fathers and brothers to military service and for the first time since the foundation of the State, Irish soldiers would serve overseas under their country's flag and under the blue flag of the United Nations. One of them was Anthony Browne. Although he and I attended different schools, our families knew each other, and our mothers were friends. He was a slight, agile whippet of a lad but to me he was a titan. Sadly, Anthony's deployment to the Congo in 1960 was his first and last journey overseas. His name is remembered for two reasons: he was part of an Irish peacekeeping unit on patrol in an African jungle when he was killed by the Baluba tribe in the infamous Niemba ambush and he was awarded a BMC - the Military Medal for Gallantry, posthumously.

Anthony Browne and some of the older boys in our locality were my heroes, particularly those who had joined the army. Their status rose to dizzying heights when the first Irish UN peacekeepers went to the Congo in 1960. Every six months, the buzz of excitement grew as the Congo dominated the news. Boys were coming home in uniform, looking grown up, sun-tanned and fit. I wanted to be like them. There was talk of 'medicals' to be passed: 'inspections' and doctors and 'inoculations', but none of that put me off.

Many years earlier, as a very young child I was admitted to the Meath Hospital to have my tonsils out. I have no memory of my stay in hospital, but I do remember the burning, post-surgery pain for which the standard treatment was ice cream. At around age twelve I was again admitted to the Meath Hospital for a month, with what was said to be 'a touch of rheumatics.' I was plunged into a daily routine that began at dawn with a round of examinations, the taking of temperatures and the administration of drugs. I can still remember the horrible after-taste of the thermometer in my mouth. The movement of bowels was of vital importance. If bowels had not moved, an enema of warm, soapy water was delivered via a long tube, a very painful and uncomfortable procedure – to be avoided at all cost. We soon learned that when the nurse went around to every patient and asked, "Have your bowels moved?" that answering "Yes" was the safe option. The bowel-emptying, temper-ature-taking and examination routine lasted for over an hour and breakfast of sticky porridge, when it came, was a welcome relief. Being confined to bed, I had to have a bed bath every day and I had the misfortune of being visited on two separate occasions by my aunt, Biddy. I was having a bed bath the first time she showed up and on her second visit she found me enthroned on a bed pan.

I had missed a month in school and although I worked hard, I had trouble catching up in every subject. The exception was Maths for which I seemed to have a natural aptitude. But the stay in hos-pital afforded time to indulge in two of my favourite pastimes – reading and drawing. I read *Moby Dick* and a month's worth of *The Beano* and I drew horses on sketch pads brought to me by my aunt Biddy. Those of us confined to bed amused ourselves throwing a ball from one to the other. There must have been an adult male patient in the ward, as I remember a man getting a belt of a ball in the head! As I look back, I can see that the military-type routine in the Meath Hospital prepared me for army life. When at last I went home I felt strange and out of place and I had to ease myself back into family life and back into school - not unlike returning from overseas service with the army.

I joined An Fórsa Cosanta Áitiúil (FCA) or Local Defence Force at fifteen, having lied about my age and received my early weapons training on the rifle, bayonet and grenade at Gormanston in County Meath. Historically, Gormanston was a British Army camp, handed over to the Irish National Army in 1922, and comprised two hundred and sixty acres of open, flat land between Balbriggan and Drogheda along the east coast. During these week-long training exercises, a 'field day' or sports day was held. Irish stew was served. I hated Irish stew and in consequence, a field day was a hungry day. I hated field days, but I loved the FCA.

The highlight of my year in the FCA was the Easter Parade in Dublin in 1962. Wearing World War Two helmets and carrying .303 Enfield rifles, the FCA marched behind the regular army, most of whom were now veterans of the Congo – and national heroes – saluting the dignitaries on the stand outside the General Post Office. It was one of the proudest moments of my life.

CHAPTER 2

Africa

Filled with patriotic fervour and with the Congo in my sights, joining the army in 1963 seemed like the most natural direction in which to take myself. My FCA training meant that I knew how to march and that I was an expert on the Mills-HE-hand and rifle grenade. The months between April and September 1963 seemed to fly. I was a Two-Star Private, pot-walloping, dish-washing and cleaning as well as square-bashing, button-polishing and maintaining uniform and rifle in pristine condition. I was elated to find my name on a list of Congo-bound troops and was immediately ordered to Clancy Barracks. Formerly known as Islandbridge Barracks with a long history of artillery, cavalry and ordnance, it was renamed Clancy Barracks in 1942 after Peader Clancy, a County Clare man killed in 1920, during the War of Independence. Clancy was situated on the south bank of the river Liffey just a stone's throw from my home in Rialto. My next stop would be Cathal Brugha Barracks where, aged seventeen I would train for the Congo Mission.

Trained on the FN rifle, I was in No. 3 Platoon. My platoon officer was Lieutenant Johnny Martin and the platoon sergeants were Sergeant Michael Moore and Sergeant Dan Mannix DSM whom I would later learn had played a pivotal role in 'The Battle of the Tunnel' in Elizabethville in the Congo. Another Congo veteran was Corporal 'Manono' Lynch, who was Post Commander at Niemba following the death of Lieutenant Kevin Gleeson, of the ill-fated patrol on the 8th of November 1960. Corporal Lynch never mentioned the disaster that was Niemba and we didn't ask.

My decision to enlist at seventeen years of age had required a

Form of Consent signed by my parents – mandatory for a boy under eighteen years of age. I was then a minor and the army would be acting in loco parentis. My mother was in shock. She saw the FCA as a pastime that she hoped I would outgrow. She hoped that joining the army might be a passing phase and that I would get over it. Like everyone else in the country, she had been distraught by events in the Congo – events that had come too close to home when her neighbour's son was killed in the infamous Niemba ambush. When his remains were finally found in 1962 they were repatriated and buried with military honours in Glasnevin Cemetery. She had wept for Anthony Browne's family and felt deeply for them in their loss. She could not believe that his death had not altered my decision to go to 'that awful place'.

My mother's concerns, nor the tragic events in the Congo, had much effect on me. Concerns and tragedy belonged to the adult world. I was having fun with crowds of fellow teenage lads in Cathal Brugha Barracks where I developed a taste for rib roast beef and spent much of meal times ducking as quarter loaves of bread were launched across a dining hall crammed with several hundred recruits. Punch-ups broke out regularly and were great fun. The barrack square reverberated with orders and the sound of the marching of the heavy leather hobnailed boots of four platoons. We could hear ourselves and each other marching, like a symphony orchestra, each soldier an instrument. Nowadays, soldiers cannot hear themselves marching because they have rubber boots, so they need a single drummer to beat time. To an old soldier, this is appalling!

We practiced tactics, weapons training, and the new FN rifle on firing ranges, measurement of pace, harmony in the step with the aid of a metronome and a pacing stick used by the sergeant major. After sixteen weeks and lots of rehearsals, we passed out. The Passing-Out Parade usually occurred on a Friday at 11 a.m. with a brass band and the General Officer Commanding in attendance. A happy day, a day out for the family and a proud day for our parents. We, the soldiers were especially proud, wearing our Two-Star rank marking. The following Monday, I was posted to the 5th Infantry Battalion and then, after farewells we climbed onto a Bedford 4x2 truck to join our first unit. I was posted to Collins' Barracks, Dublin. Further specialist training was required but first, I had to do a conversation course on the Lee-Enfield rifle, 0.303. My time in the FCA was paying dividends.

The high, sinister walls in Collins' Barracks created long dark shadows, but the beautiful old clock chiming during the night, ringing out the hours and half-hours gave a sense of security. We slept in a large dormitory, accommodating twenty men. Five blankets were available with cold stiff linen sheets which were also used as tablecloths and washed in the now infamous institutions that were the Magdalene Laundries. Big turf fires were kept burning. Rifles were locked in stand-up racks, the keys held by the room orderly. Bayonets were locked in a box beside the rifle rack. Rifle, bolt and bayonet all bore serial numbers. We had 'bath parade' for which a 'bath book' was maintained – a register of soldiers' washing. This process was followed by 'short-arms inspection', carried out by the medical corps. Only army medical corps personnel were present during inspection to which we had been marched by our NCOs. We had to line up in single file, wearing long shirts, so nothing was seen by comrades and one's dignity was respected in as much as it could be. Armpits and genitalia were examined but not touched. The medics were looking for any evidence of scabies, lice, and more sinister diseases like STDs. Few, if any of us knew what STDs were. Usually, the morning canteen break was next, and we were free to go for a cup of tea. This relieved the stress and discomfort of the inspection.

After breakfast, a roll call, followed by allocation of tasks such as Fatigues, or postings as orderlies to officers or officers' wives and families. In Collins Barracks there were three main households: the chaplain, the O'Catháins, and up the hill, Adjutant General, Major

General Sean Collins-Powell and his wife. Those doing courses were in a separate group, training on an 81 mm mortar or on a Vickers machine gun. I was seen as a 'nice boy' and I was given duties at all three houses. One soldier who was sent to Major General Sean Collin-Powell's wife wasn't too keen on work. "What would you be doing in the Barracks?" Mrs. Collins-Powell asked him. "Nothing, Ma'am, lying on my bed". The lady reported this to her husband who informed Brigade Headquarters and the officer commanding the 5th Infantry Battalion. Thereafter, there were surprise inspections of billets and lots of room inspections, inspections of kit and lockers and could include foot inspections by the platoon officer. Infantry soldiers must have good, clean feet and socks. If one's boots became smelly they were to be burned because the smell would transfer onto washed – and even new – socks. I was about to escape overseas, and I hoped that on my return, all would have returned to normal.

There were three messes in Collins' Barrack – an officers' mess, a sergeants' and corporals' mess and a fourth one for soldiers. Soldiers who were not on courses or who were on household duty or Fatigues invariably ended up in one of the messes, washing dishes, cutlery and pots. One sergeant in the dining hall used a large block of carbolic soap which he held under scalding water with a meat skewer and the suds cascaded over cups, saucers and plates. Soldiers had their own cutlery. In the field, they had metal plates known as 'mess tins'.

Breakfast was from 8 a.m. to 8.30 a.m. There could be several hundred soldiers for breakfast and dining hall orderly duty required one to awake earlier than one's peers, set tables with cups and saucers and leave out bread, sugar, butter and a jug of milk. Each table seated four, so four quarters of bread and four half-ounce pieces of butter were laid out. One very fussy sergeant would take a random sample of cups laid out after breakfast for dinner and if he found one dirty cup, everything had to be re-washed. Leftovers were dumped into the swill which was collected daily by the 'pig man' who smelled to high heaven. Once a month the pig man paid the command welfare officer for the swill. This contract was tendered for – and highly sought after.

The work in the officers' mess was done by civilian waiters and a civilian chef. The corporals' mess was another matter. On Sundays we had casual meals for civilians who had been elected as associate members. One of the cooks, if stuck, would go to the swill bucket and remove bits of meat, wash them under the tap, return them to the plate and pour gravy over them. One day I was detailed to go the sergeants' mess after a 'crubeen party'. There were pigs' feet everywhere, behind pictures – even in the pockets of the snooker table. Close to the dining hall was the turf depot, complete with a horse and cart. The horse had a service number and a medical book! Turf was collected in kit bags and carried to fire places across to the units and staffs in barracks. Room orderlies did this work, as did soldiers on Fatigues duty. The standard of cleanliness was very high, to avoid infection. Hygiene was uppermost. Like my father, I liked order and discipline. I strove for perfection and I excelled at all tasks – big and small.

Excitement grew when preparations for the visit of President John F. Kennedy began. I was honoured to be selected as part of the military guard of honour lining the route for the Kennedy cavalcade procession through the centre of the city. Hours before 'Air Force One' touched down at Dublin Airport, the city of Dublin came to a standstill. Kennedy stood in the open-topped limousine, wearing a blue suit, his sandy hair copper highlighted by the summer sun and a permanent broad smile on his face as he waved to the crowds. At the Leaders' graveside in Arbour Hill, the 36th Cadet Class performed the Funeral Drill. The drill made such an impression on the President that he spoke about it ad nauseam on his return to the United States. We had practiced this Funeral Drill too, as part of our training.

The cheers of the crowds lining the route were still ringing in my ears as I presented myself at St. Bricin's Hospital in Arbour Hill to have a vaccination against smallpox and a troublesome tooth extracted. This necessitated forty-eight hours' excused duty (ED) and I found myself confined to nearby Collins Barracks while in recovery, itching to be on the move. Finally, I was summoned by the sergeant major, a kind, crusty old man. "Take off your shirt and turn right," he ordered. The marks on my arm, left by the smallpox vaccination were clearly visible. "Right," he said. "Pack your kit, you're going to the Congo." My whole body tingled with excitement and I floated out the door on a cloud.

We then travelled to the Curragh Military Camp, a former British Army camp where we were accommodated in long, large billets on the first floor of old buildings which at one time were used as stables for the horses. We washed while standing on cold, slate flooring and the water was freezing. No showers. It was primitive compared to the snug rooms and bathing area occupied by commissioned officers. We trained Mondays to Fridays so at least we could bathe at home at weekends. There was a cinema in the Curragh, flea-ridden and to be avoided. We did weapons training in the Glen of Imaal, high in the Wicklow Mountains, on ranges for heavy weapons – mortars, artillery, and armoured cars. The Glen was a form of purgatory, a rite of passage so to speak – a hungry location, with terrible food. We were accommodated in billets with pot-belly stoves for heating and a 'drying room', operated by a civilian. Washing facilities were outside, as were the toilets. Imaal was mainly about bonding and hardships shared.

Our pay was poor, just enough to buy cigarettes. I was addicted. I would buy a week's supply at a time. But, I believed I was the bees' knees, trained for battle, ready to face the enemy – Balubas, mercenaries – whatever the Congo could throw at us. My recruit platoon sergeant seemed to think otherwise. "McQuaid, you're a timid little bastard who could do with a good kick up the arse!" he roared. But within a few weeks the 'timid little bastard' was wearing the blue beret with the United Nations emblem and standing, shoulders back, head high in the line-up of the 2nd Infantry Group for review by the Taoiseach, Seán Lemass.

Our deployment in late November 1963 would bring Ireland's involvement in the Congo mission to an end. Our reputation preceded us; our troops had put Ireland on the map at the highest level. President John F. Kennedy's speech to the Irish houses of Parliament, just a few months earlier had left no-one in any doubt that we were in the vanguard of the struggle for world peace. "I am glad, therefore, that Ireland is moving in the mainstream of current world events," he said. "For I sincerely believe that your future is as promising as your past is proud, and that your destiny lies not as a peaceful island in a sea of troubles but as a maker and shaper of world peace. Twenty-six sons of Ireland have died in the Congo; many others have been wounded. Their sacrifice reminds us all that we must not falter now. I pay tribute to them and to all of you for your commitment and dedication to world order".

Kennedy's great-grandparents had left Ireland for America in the 1840s to escape the Irish famine. They settled in Massachusetts where his grandfather and father were born into a family that quickly established itself in business in a highly sectarian society, where Irish Catholics were excluded by upper-class Bostonians. The Boston Irish became active in the Democratic Party and P. J. Kennedy, the patriarch of the Kennedy family was an accomplished businessman who provided a comfortable lifestyle for family. His son, John, no doubt eager to maintain the voting power of the Irish in America and with the patriotic Irish blood coursing through his veins, sent a strong message to the world from the podium in the Houses of the Oireachtas in Dublin that the might of the American Dollar would be placed at Ireland's disposal. "Ireland's influence in the United Nations is far greater than your relative size," Kennedy said. "You have not hesitated to take the lead on such sensitive issues as the Kashmir dispute and you sponsored that most vital resolution, adopted by the General Assembly, which opposed the spread of nuclear arms to any nation not now possessing them, urging an international agreement with inspection and control, and I pledge to you that the United States of America will do all in its power to achieve such an agreement and fulfil your resolution".

The United States Air Force had already been pressed into service at the beginning of the Congo campaign. U.S. aircraft and crew were a frequent sight at Baldonnel, the crew watching with much amusement, the young Irish troops clad in heavy bulls wool uniforms and hobnailed boots, heading for the tropics. "A couple of them asked us if we were going to the North Pole," a veteran said in an interview, fifty years later. The equipment too must have drawn a smile or two: WW1-issue rifles, the ubiquitous Bedford trucks that had seen better days and the tin cans that passed for armoured cars. These Ford armoured fighting vehicles (AFVs) had been manufactured in a CIE bus-building workshop in Tullamore during World War Two. The problem was, they weren't armoured, just soft steel. Calling them "fighting vehicles" was stretching the imagination. The turret mounted a water-cooled Vickers .303 MMG from World War One. It was fired by pulling two handles and was fixed internally at the three and nine o'clock positions and rotated the turret. This required a strong physical effort which was made more difficult when standing on empty cartridge cases that, during action, littered the floor of the car. The gunner had to stand up when sighting the gun which was particularly difficult for small gunners who had to use ammunition boxes to stand on. There were no optics and it was impossible to rotate and fire at the same time. However, because of the high skills level of the crews, these cars had greatly outperformed their specifications at many of the locations where the troops were engaged in battle.

The Americans stifled giggles at the proliferation of holy scapulars, 'miraculous' medals, Rosary beads and saints' relics that were draped around the necks of the boys in bulls wool, becoming entangled in the dog-tags or snagged on tunic buttons. More of this paraphernalia was pressed into their free hands and into their tunic pockets by their Irish Catholic mothers. The US airmen must have pitied their innocence – and balked at our ignorance as a nation. Three years later, the giant Globemaster and Hercules troop carriers that had transported the first battalions to the Congo had lifted off from Baldonnel Aerodrome in west Dublin had been replaced by Boeing 707s that operated out of Dublin Airport by Sabena Airlines of Belgium. With a long tradition of service to African destinations, Sabena also held thirty percent of the shares in the newly established Air Congo. In these modern aircraft we had proper seating and pressurised cabins, a lot more comfort than that endured by the troops in the rumbling troop carriers that had a maximum cruising height of eighteen thousand feet, in which soldiers had been deafened by the engine noise, many of them vomiting their way across two continents in 1960 and 1961. But by June 1963, this implausible army had made its mark. On his visit to Dublin, Kennedy was greeted by a very different Ireland. And he wanted us to know that the world knew. "I speak of these matters today not because Ireland is unaware of its role, but I think it important that you know that we know what you have done, and I speak to remind the other small nations that they too can – and must help build a world peace". It had barely been a blink of an eye – just a short time after we had settled into our routine in Kolwezi, Congo, when we heard the news that John F. Kennedy was dead. His widow, Jacqueline requested that Irish cadets travel to Arlington Cemetery to perform the Funeral Drill at his graveside and the 37th Cadet class boarded a special flight from Dublin to Washington and made Irish Military history.

Our dead were heroes. The tragedy of Niemba had plunged the nation into grief and elevated the victims to sainthood. The triumph of the 36th Battalion at the 'Battle of the Tunnel' in 1961 had received wide coverage, both inside the Irish Defence Forces and in the public media. A young officer, Lieutenant Paddy Riordan and his Radio Man, Private Andy Wickham had died in the early stages of the battle and Sergeant Paddy Mulcahy had died later from his wounds. But among these heroes was a whole company of Irish soldiers had been kept from the limelight. Their suffering and bravery would be swept under the carpet – because they had surrendered. Their pleas for justice would fall on deaf ears. While the UN, our country's President and Chief of Staff, Éamon DeValera, the Irish government and those at the top of the defence forces' pyramid did everything they could to maintain silence, the soldiers of A Company, 35th Battalion, the 'boots on the ground' – the most vulnerable – suffered ridicule and shame. Their week-long ordeal in a small mining town called Jadotville, hewn out of an African jungle, was dismissed and their surrender seen as an embarrassment. These young men were left to deal in whatever way they could with their nightmares in the aftermath of that event. Their gallant commanding officer, Commandant Pat Quinlan was hauled before committees to give an account of himself, but the truth was too hot for them to handle. Had Lieutenant Kevin Gleeson survived the massacre at Niemba in 1960 he too would have been hung out to dry to conceal the shortcomings of his superiors and the UN elite. Unlike Pat Quinlan and the men of the 35th however, he and eight of his little patrol were spared disgrace and betrayal by virtue of gruesome deaths.

The Congo campaign had claimed twenty-six young lives. Their sacrifice and the bravery and competence of the thousands that had served had left a quieter Congo for our 2nd Infantry Group now patrolling the Angolan border. We were living in tents, lulled to sleep at night by the sound of crickets – once we got used to it. The crickets and other insects played the evening symphony, a cacophony of sounds. Forked lighting danced across the sky at night, rain storms flooded the drainage channels and we could soap and shower in the swollen rivers. Women with barrels on their heads and children in slings on their backs walked along the side of the road in single file for fear of being killed by a white man driving a car. We joked that the Congo was not a place to die; bodies would decompose very quickly.

At seventeen, I was the youngest soldier in the company. My best friend was Dominic Doyle from Gowran in Kilkenny. We became accustomed to calling each other by our numbers instead of our names. This was how we were roll-called on morning parade. I was Number 11; he Number 20. "How's Eleven?" Dominic would say. "How's Twenty?" I would answer. Parades to Mass, call-outs, patrols, rain, floods and beer-drinking punctuated our days and at times, our nights. Afternoon siestas were obligatory. We could speak directly to corporals, never to sergeants or officers. Officers only addressed lowest ranks during formal inspection parades and usually to comment on some aspect of dress.

My mother and I wrote letters to each other regularly. She sent me a Christmas pudding – which must be still travelling! I was missing my mother and missing my siblings, especially my youngest brother, now aged nine. I had practically reared him from the day my mother brought him home from the National Maternity Hospital. I had almost lost him when as a toddler in my care, he had fallen into the canal. Like my father, who rescued a man from the canal in 1954, I jumped in and fished him out. My fate, had he drowned, was probably too terrible to contemplate! Although homesick I could never speak of homesickness; it just wasn't the done thing. Besides, I was all grown up now. I was a soldier – an Irish soldier. I had an FN rifle and I was mandated by my country and by the United Nations to keep the peace in a country the size of Europe that had been hell bent on self-destruction.

Our first – and only – drama occurred when the baker stopped baking bread, the trusted staple that supplemented our army rations of tinned soup, potatoes, tinned meat and anything the cook could buy from the locals. The reason for the baker's strike remained a mystery for some days and then it emerged that his wife had been raped. Like many of my fellow Irish lads, I was too young and ignorant to understand the meaning of rape. It was the absence of fresh bread that gave cause for much of our grumbling. "Politics" was the reason the baker's wife was raped, we were told.

Politics had led us here. A mutiny started on July 4th, 1960, only four days after the Congo, hitherto a Belgian colony was granted Independence. The Congolese troops had their own ideas about the meaning of an independent democratic republic. The soldiers broke into the armoury and with guns, ammunition and machetes, turned on their white, Belgian officers. Eight days later all one thousand Belgian officers had been killed or removed from their positions. With no officer corps, the soldiers ran amok throughout the Congo and panic-stricken whites were fleeing in all directions. Three years later, Belgian homes, schools, hospitals and businesses were still being attacked. The UN, seen as a force that supported unification of the Congo, was initially despised and still mistrusted. By this time, plane-loads of Belgians had fled the country while others, like the baker and his wife who were Belgian tried to ignore the precarious nature of the civil war, believing that they were safe in Katanga Province which had seceded from the rest of the Congo after Independence. The fact that the baker was supplying UN troops had made had him a target.

Despite this, our routine had to be maintained. Call-outs could happen at any time of the day or night and we had to rest whenever the opportunity arose. Medics patrolled the camp between noon and three p.m. to make sure that we got our heads down. I discovered 'Simba', the local beer, encouraged by the 'old sweats' – eighteen-to-twenty-years-olds – who were already seasoned drinkers. Finally, we moved from our station at 'Camp Ruwe', a former school, run by missionary priests, to Company Headquarters in Kolwezi to assist in preparing stores for repatriation. We were in an area that had been bulldozed for tents in which we slept on iron beds that had probably been hospital beds in a previous existence. On pay-day we made a beeline for the American PX (stores). We bought souvenirs by the truck-load. 'Mingies' – bows and arrows, spears, knives and wooden carved figurines constituted the bulk of our luggage on our way home – Congo art that still decorates man-telpieces, shelves, walls or gathers dust in the attics of the homes of Congo veterans across Ireland to this day. Omega watches were the most popular purchases but a beautiful Roamer Rotodate watch caught my eye. Fifty-seven years later I still have it.

In the days before repatriation we were accommodated in a for-mer grain store in the town of Elizabethville, where much of the fighting between the UN and Katangese, Congolese and hired mer-cenaries from all over the world had taken place between 1961 and 1962. But as we waited for our time to go home, boredom and idleness led to consumption of alcohol by the (army-issue) mugful and stomachs were soon protesting. Rats the size of cats, unper-turbed by the stench of stale vomit, patrolled the steel girders above our heads. Undeterred and fortified by a few square meals, we spent two drunken nights in Kano, Nigeria, while waiting for some repairs to our aircraft. We stopped again in Rome and overnighted there before the final leg of the journey home. I had turned eigh-teen, I was still a Two-Star Private but a Two-Star Private with a Congo medal. I was ten feet tall. After the routine one month's leave I returned to duties and completed my Young Entry Course on the Vickers machine gun and was upgraded to a Three-Star Pri-vate. My dream of going to the Congo had been fulfilled. I felt rewarded for what I had achieved on the Young Entry Course and I was eager for more learning and adventure. My excitement knew no bounds when I was accepted for duty with the 41st Infantry Battalion in Cyprus.

CHAPTER 3

Descent into Hell

Nothing I cared, in the lamb white days,
that time would take me
Up to the swallow thronged loft by the shadow of my hand,
In the moon that is always rising,
Nor that riding to sleep
I should hear him fly with the high fields
And wake to the farm forever fled from the childless land.
Oh as I was young and easy in the mercy of his means,
Time held me green and dying
Though I sang in my chains like the sea.

Fern Hill, Dylan Thomas

Cyprus had been declared a British crown colony in 1925. Like the Irish, many Greek and Turkish Cypriots fought in the British Army during both world wars. When Britain refused to grant self-determination to Cyprus in the 1950s, the Greek Cypriots demanded *enosis* (union with Greece). In 1960 a treaty of guarantee, signed by Cyprus, Greece, Turkey and the United Kingdom was regarded by both the Greek and Turkish Cypriots as provisional. Secretly, the Greek Cypriots, under Archbishop Makarios intended to amend the constitution in their favour, suppress Turkish Cypriot resistance and declare enosis. With discontent on both sides, nationalist militants, with the military support of Greece and Turkey respectively started training again. Violence erupted just days before Christmas, 1963 when two Turkish Cypriots were killed during an incident involving the Greek Cypriot police. The violence resulted in the

24

deaths of hundreds of Turkish and Greek Cypriots, the destruction of over a hundred villages and the displacement of between twenty thousand and thirty thousand Turkish Cypriots. In some areas, Greek Cypriots prevented Turkish Cypriots from travelling or entering government buildings. Turkish Cypriots began living in enclaves and the capital, Nicosia was divided by a 'Green Line' with the deployment of UNFICYP troops, the Irish among them. The mission in Cyprus had three main aims: to prevent the recurrence of fighting; to help maintain law and order and to contribute to the restoration of normal life for the Cypriot people.

I gleaned smatterings of information about Cyprus from the media news, on the army grapevine from troops already on duty there and from old travel brochures. I knew Famagusta and Nicosia, exotic names that stuck. Famagusta was the number one tourist destination. The summer temperatures were exceedingly hot and between the middle of June and the middle of September most Cypriots didn't venture outside between eleven in the morning and four in the afternoon because of the scorching heat. The landscape varied from large open bays along the coast, rising to tree-covered mountains with fertile hilly country in between. Famagusta had many new high-rise buildings and hotels to cater for the increasing number of tourists, but just hours before the Greek Cypriot and Turkish armies clashed in military combat on the streets of Famagusta, the entire population of the city fled. Irish troops of the 40th Battalion had already served in Famagusta on the east coast of Cyprus. In the depths of winter, we would be relieving them.

Every other day I inspected my arms to see if hair would grow on them, in high spirits, too young to understand the complexities of international political conflict or how it translated into the lives of ordinary people. I knew that we were heading into a danger area and that there had been fighting, but I trusted our officers to tell us where to go and what to do and if necessary, our weapons would protect us from danger in the field.

We arrived in Cyprus on the 31st of October 1964 and were stationed at Famagusta, in a British camp that we called 'Camp Luxury'. By our standards, it was summer in Cyprus. We went swimming every day and my Congo sun tan was steadily deepening. The walled city of Famagusta, with the Othello Tower, the harbour and the docks, was still very beautiful. We had good accommodation and fish and chip vans called to 'Famagee' at night. I can still smell the vinegar! The 'Egyptian's house' was used as the Platoon HQ and when I arrived to take up my position as the platoon commander's orderly, two large German Shepherd dogs hurled themselves towards me. For a moment, nothing but fresh air hung between me and a pair of open, salivating jaws. Just inches from my legs, a sharp whistle brought them to a skidding halt and the dogs slinked back into the shadows. I was shaken but recovered in time to present myself for duty.

As the platoon commander's orderly I had to follow him everywhere, like a personal housemaid, with never ending duties including washing his underwear. But I loved it there and this tour of duty looked as if it would be as enjoyable as the Congo had been, until the battalion was given a 'warning order' to move to the Morphou area, north of Famagusta – cold and mountainous terrain. Our company, A Company, was assigned the Limnitis area, essentially a bog-hole with mud everywhere. We set up camp, accommodated in four-man tents on cots for beds, with gravel underneath. Oil lamps were provided and three extra blankets. Later on, we acquired oil stoves to keep us warm.

I was very glad to be liberated from the boredom of orderly duties. But danger was all around, and we could never let our guard down. Travel was dangerous for civilians. We watched them closely, making sure that they would not be kidnapped and killed in our area. Tobacco growers and farmers worked hard and used donkeys to carry heavy loads along the mountain tracks. Human faeces, used as fertiliser on the barren fields, and slaughtered cattle, hanging by the legs in market stalls in the villages took some getting used to. Our food and water were scarce, and we were glad to exit the Limnitis hell-hole for the OPS duty, high in the hills, for fourteen days at a time. Although it could be a very lonely eight-hour shift on OPS duty, it was better than being in camp and the reveille, bugle calls, parades, inspection, drill, weapons-training, guard duty, spit-and-polish, filling sandbags and the nightly shout, 'Lights Out' at bedtime routine. We found that the Turkish Cypriots were friendly and hospitable. On one occasion, I was deeply touched when a Turkish Cypriot night watchman shared his small meal of bread and cauliflower with me.

After the cold and rain of autumn and winter, everywhere was green in spring. Back at base, free time passed playing cards, playing volley ball or hanging out with friends in neighbouring tents. I was partial to a couple of bottles of Simba in the Congo, but Simba was not a feature of life in Cyrus and I wasn't drawn to sampling any other brand. My addiction to cigarettes consumed my per diem from the UN. We were accumulating 'credits' at home but were not encouraged to draw down our credits except for something special. For the first time I heard about 'red light districts', of which there was apparently no shortage in Nicosia. We were given the names of the streets in these areas and advised to avoid them. Most of the troops did. The married lads were faithful to their wives and most of those that were unmarried were terrified of contracting 'a dose' and carrying it home.

In February, I learned that we had a four days' leave time due and that it would entail a tour of the Holy Land. The Holy Land was considered special and to an Irish Catholic boy, full of religious zeal, a chance to visit the land that Jesus came from was too good to be missed. I boarded the ME Airlines Viscount with high expectations, born of nineteen years' prayers, memories of the smell of fresh straw from the Christmas crib: the 'manger' that was said to have housed the Holy Family on the night that Jesus was born. I was familiar with images of the wise men, sometimes called 'the three kings': men in long robes who had followed the star to Bethlehem to pay homage to the Infant Jesus and the images of large crucifixes bearing the image of His naked body with the flesh wound in His side that hung in every church. None of my friends seemed interested in going on the trip to Jerusalem but I knew a couple of the lads from another unit, Privates Francis Byrne and Tom Browne who were going. The rest of the unit I knew only by sight or by name.

Our flight circumnavigated Israel as parts of the Holy Land were not accessible to us. We flew to Beirut and from there to Jordan where I noticed crowds of people kneeling on mats on the ground, all of them facing in one direction. Every now and then they would rise up and then prostrate themselves again, all the while praying aloud. I learned that they had to pray facing Mecca. We were in the home of Islam, ruled by the House of Hashim, known as the Hashemites who ruled Mecca continuously from the 10th century until its conquest by the House of Saud in 1924. Their ancestor was Hashim ibn Abd Manaf, great-grandfather of the Islamic prophet, Muhammed. The crowd, praying and chanting was exotic. This is what I expected The Holy Land to be like.

On our arrival in Jerusalem we were bussed to our hotel. The streets smelled of incense and the pungent aromas of the spice market filled the hot, dry air. Our hotel was within walking distance of some of the most famous sites. Other sites were a longer journey away by bus. In a courtyard, we disembarked into the still warm, late afternoon. We were accommodated four to a room. By modern standards, the hotel would be basic but to a bunch of young men from Ireland, used to roughing it in a military camp, a bed with real bedclothes and the smell of meat and chips were luxury. I was delighted to be here in the land where Christ walked. I would walk in His footsteps and pray in temples built by caliphs and kings. The cold and the rain of Limnitis had faded, the stress of constant high-alert status was beginning to ease, and the warmth felt good.

I had just entered a toilet, next to the bar when one of our corporals came through the door behind me. I had seen him on the flight and later on the bus but did not know him previously. While undoing his zipper and without a word, he pushed my face against the wall. Immediately, his hand gripped my penis, shaking, pulling, squeezing. Then he violently penetrated me. Brutal. Bestial. Searing pain shot up along my spine. Breath left me. I dropped to my knees, my head throbbing my stomach nauseous, my heart pounding like a drum in my ears. My legs trembled, my hands clawed the floor. Life left me, and the world went black. When I came to, his sticky semen was congealing, clinging to my buttocks and I could feel warm blood running down the inside of my thighs – my own blood. My tongue had swollen in my mouth. A pool of tears had gathered on the floor.

Somehow, I manage to stand. I am trembling, fumbling with shoe laces…removing my shoes and trousers…stepping out of my soiled underpants…wiping off blood and his contamination. I am pulling on my trousers again…forcing my feet into my shoes… removing my shirt. I stagger to a washbasin and scoop water into my mouth and onto my face and neck, sweat pumping through every pore. The journey to my room has faded from my memory.

As soon as I lay down on my bed, the trembling in my legs returned. They now felt distorted and swollen. My head felt like it was wrapped tightly in bandages and my pelvis, from hip to hip, felt as if it had been ripped asunder. I could hear no sound. I was beginning to feel cold and numb. I couldn't make my hands move and the room had become blurred. Nothing seemed familiar. Suddenly I was floating out of my body. I struggled to come back but I was afraid of the pain throbbing all along my spine, something like gravel behind my eyes, the sickness in my stomach, wanting to retch but couldn't. I hung, suspended above my body for God knows how long. Eventually I passed out.

I was awoken by bright sunlight. Its harshness hurt my eyes. As the events of the previous evening began to come back into focus, my stomach, still convulsing, felt as if it wanted to burst out from inside my body. Through eyes that could barely open, I looked around the room. The other beds were empty; my room mates had already left for breakfast. I remembered that we were going on a bus tour that had been arranged by the welfare officer. Then, suddenly, *he*, the assailant was there, standing in the room. Fear swept through me. "How'ya," he said, grinning. "You coming on the tour?" "Fuck off," I shouted. I had never in my life used such language. I heard the words fall out of my mouth, not believing that I was actually uttering them. He laughed, turned on his heel and left. A few minutes later another corporal walked in. "Come on, get downstairs," he ordered. "You're holding up the bus!" So used to obeying orders, I swung my legs out of bed and tried to stand but my knees buckled and I hit the floor. On all fours, I tried to breathe, but breathing was a struggle and a wave of dizziness swept over me. My stomach heaved but nothing came up.

I made it downstairs as far as the terrace. A waiter was standing off to one side. His eyes met mine as I gripped the edge of a small table, to steady myself and flopped onto a chair in the shade. He immediately followed me and sat right next to me at the table. Although I was wearing a white fleece jacket that my friend, Corporal Doyle had loaned me before leaving Cyprus, I was shivering. My head hurt, my groin and lower spine throbbed in pain.

The corporal who had ordered me downstairs approached, leaned across the table and ordered me onto the bus. "I'm not getting on the bus with that man on it," I said. "What are you talking about, McQuaid? Get on the bus – now!" I told him what had happened the night before in the toilet. He paused. I was glued to the chair, trembling. The waiter leaned forward as if preparing to place himself between the corporal and myself. I had a feeling that the waiter knew something. Maybe he had heard noises during the attack. Had I cried out? Had he seen the attacker leave afterwards? I was too weak to ask.

Private Browne appeared at the corporal's shoulder. I heard the click of a camera button. The corporal moved away. The waiter lingered but he did not speak. I needed to get away from there. When the bus left, I got to my feet and began to walk unsteadily towards the gate. I walked and walked towards the streets in a stupor, stumbling, half consciousness, still in pain, still bleeding. Apart from children asking for 'Baksheesh', I have no memory of what I was doing. I was apart from the world.

I have no recollection of returning to the hotel. From then on, time would hold me, 'green and dying'. Days later, when Browne had his photographs developed he distributed them among the rest of us. In one photograph, the corporal is standing over me. The waiter is sitting next to me with a wary eye on the cameraman. I guessed that he had probably heard sounds in the toilet and I strongly suspected that he knew what had happened to me. But he never spoke.

From then on, I was unable to eat. I kept going to the bathroom to wash, then to bed. During the night I drifted in and out of sleep. Each time I awoke it was from a nightmare. Relief on waking was momentary; the light from the hotel corridor shining through the fanlight over the door told me that this was reality. On the third day, I dragged myself out of bed and tagged along with Private Tom Browne and a few of the others. Another photographer took a photo of Francis Byrne and me kneeling in the Church of the Nativity at the birthplace of Jesus in Bethlehem. It all seemed surreal. I had no life left in me. I was not engaging in banter any more. I could barely speak at all. It was as if I was watching a bad film – in black and white – that played the same scenes over and over: the attack in the toilet blending with another historical site. The Dome of the Rock, more photographs. Onto the bus. Off the bus. At any moment I thought I would wake up, but I was a walking dead person.

Private Browne was making the most of the location and the sights to create photographic memories of the tour. He asked some of us to pose for photographs, at the tomb of Lazarus and at other landmarks. I agreed, simply to be sociable and appear to act normally. Not having brought a change of underwear on this trip, I did not have a clean pair to replace the pair that had been soiled during the assault and in the photographs, I am self-conscious and very uncomfortable because I am not wearing any underwear. Each photograph serves only to remind me of my state of debilitation and torment. Some years ago, the wife of a friend was looking through the old photographs. When she looked at the photograph taken at the tomb of Lazarus, she said, "Chris, you looked very sick. Look at the bags under your eyes!"

I was nineteen years of age, thousands of miles from home, a soldier proficient in weaponry and drill, with a good head for mathematics. Not long before then, one of my training officers called me 'a timid little bastard'. Maybe it was my youth and this timidity that flashed 'Innocence' and 'Vulnerability' like a neon sign in the night sky and prevented my voice from calling out and my limbs from running away or lashing out in self-defence. Nothing in my army training had prepared me for what happened in Jerusalem, in February 1965. When the tour ended we flew to Beirut and the Roman ruins at Baalbek and spent four days in Lebanon. On board the Viscount back to Cyprus three people knew what had happened to me in Jerusalem. One of them was the assailant.

Five days later I was back with my platoon. Manning observation posts was torture. Every now and then, the slideshow of images from Jerusalem would bring on a bout of nausea. Although my physical pain and discomfort slowly subsided it was a supreme effort to drag my attention to my surroundings and the task at hand. Back at the camp, it was the hard, physical labour and light-hearted banter amongst the unit that helped to keep me going. In the weeks that followed, we had to carry out basic drainage so that we could improve conditions at the camp. We had no foul weather clothing until we acquired some used rain gear from the United States forces. This added to the bitter complaining about accommodation, food and hard work that took my mind off my pain. The physical effort consumed my energy, so that when I lay down I could escape in sleep. I spoke to no-one about the assault and none of my superiors approached me. I met the corporal whom I had told about it a couple of times afterwards, but he never mentioned it. By day, I carried out my duties. Then, the nightmares began to take hold in darkness. The shock had given way to anger and nothing would make it go away. One morning, after an all-night shift on OPS I returned to the tent I shared with three colleagues. There was no-one around. I flung myself onto my bed. I could hardly breathe. Waves of heat swept through me. Instinctively, I began to masturbate, copying the way in which I had been manhandled by the rapist. The result was a fit of convulsions. I regretted that I hadn't blown my head off while I'd had the chance.

As summer approached, I watched the apple trees coming into bloom and knew that we would be going home soon. Finally, our six months' tour of duty was nearing an end. On the day of our departure, hungry and cold, we had to wait for four hours at the airport for our plane to arrive. No-one knew where the officers were; they didn't appear until it was time to depart. Homeward bound, I carried a deep, dark secret of violation and shame, feeling my stomach and chest tightening as the plane approached Dublin. At home, I could hardly speak to anyone. I had immediately applied to return to Cyprus. I knew the drill in the army. I could hide from the world in the force and by working hard, I could keep the torment at bay. I had people there with whom I could relate on a light-hearted, superficial level and I now knew how to be on my guard; for much of the time I would have a weapon and I would use it. I also knew that I would never sleep soundly overseas but the only solution to my torment seemed to lie in getting away again.

While I waited for my month's leave to be up, I stayed in my bedroom playing darts and listening to Roy Orbison records. I played 'Only the Lonely' over and over, an apt accompaniment to my own loneliness as I sank deeper and deeper into morbidity. Whenever I ventured out I avoided buses, not wanting to be seen. Instead, I took taxis to and from pubs in the city. In one pub I swilled down a glass of beer and gripped the glass so tightly that it broke into pieces in my hand. "Jesus!" the barman exclaimed as blood pumped from the cuts on my palm.

The 41st Infantry Battalion was replaced by the 42nd Infantry Battalion. I was with the 5th Infantry Group who arrived in Cyprus on the 24th of October 1965 and moved from Lefka to Limnitis, Kokkina, Kato Pyrgos and Xeros. Its OPS were Foxtrot, Juliet, India, Hotel and Kilo. It also had Ghaziverian and Limekiln. I soon settled into the routine, glad to be back overseas among soldiers, although at times we were more like boy scouts, away on a long camping adventure. The ever-present banter and the pranks played on one another were my saviour. I went again with the 7th Infantry Group and arrived in October 1966. We returned to the same scenario: toileting on planks fixed across deep holes in the ground that were christened 'the long drops'. The bugler with the 7th Infantry Group was in constant practice which eventually got on everyone's nerves. A couple of soldiers grabbed the bugle and threw it down a 'long drop'. Josh Keenan, the bugler was furious. During a search of the erstwhile sewer, I spotted it. "I see it, I see it!" I shouted. The green tassel had not sunk into the sludge and Sergeant John Barnes fetched a long tent pole and managed to rescue the instrument that now had a liberal coating of shit – inside and outside. Josh looked, with a mixture of disgust and heartbreak at his beloved bugle. "I'm never, ever playing that again," he announced and walked away. However, John Barnes dropped it in a fire bucket and the medics were given the job of cleaning and sterilizing the instrument. When they returned it to Josh, he examined it carefully, then raised it to his lips. Bugling began again. I submitted the story to a weekly Company magazine with an accompanying cartoon, drawn with a sewing needle on wax paper. The following week 'The Bugle' was the cover story. Josh, a wonderful musician and a lovely man later became a sergeant major.

It being winter, cold, rain and hunger were our main companions. When the long, narrow mountain road was turned to mud by rain we were transported to our observation post by a British helicopter. Again, the OPS post sustained us in that it offered an escape from the boredom of routine at the base. In Limnitis there were two check-points, one above our camp and one in the next village. At dawn, cars assembled to be brought through the Turkish Zone towards Karavostasi, a seaside town with a port which was historically used for exporting copper for which Cyprus was once famous, six kilometres north of Lefka. The soldier on check-point duty, logged the model, registration number and the number of occupants in each vehicle. A UN landrover with armed UN personnel would lead the convoy of vehicles, with another land rover taking up the rear – again with armed UN soldiers. Escort vehicles would also take cars from the other town at a pre-arranged time. This operation was to ensure that cars were not apprehended by the other side and the occupants killed. This was happening all over the mission area. A vicious hatred existed between the Greek and Turkish Cypriots and these people could, at any moment begin killing each other without mercy – and killing us in the process. We worked from 6 a.m. until twilight. It was a long day for the soldier on check-point duty, on high alert at all times. OPS were different – static – to look out for encroachments, then back to base. All check point and OPS reports would eventually find their way to UN HQ in New York.

Between OPS duties I occupied my mind by doing crosswords and I ran crossword competitions for which I had to beg prizes from the canteen manager. The British Royal Engineer Corps had helped with the excavations for the camp and they integrated with our unit. Every two weeks they came with two Bedford trucks, one kitted out as a shower, the other carrying the water. The Brits were a jolly bunch, partial to a sing-song in the evenings. They liked to sing old music hall songs and these impromptu, raucous sing-songs were a godsend. In contrast, mission hours on check-point duty were lonely, counting the hours until the ration truck came. We were sometimes visited on OPS duty by Greeks or Turks. The youngsters took a great interest in our wristwatches. They would grab our arm and gaze at the watch. When they grabbed my arm, I held my breath, not knowing if a knife or a dagger would suddenly appear! Maybe I imagined it. At this stage, my imagination was running away with me. Holding myself together had become difficult. The line between reality and a state of displacement blurred. Something awful had happened to me and the strain of holding and keeping a terrible, grotesque and shameful secret under wraps at all times was often all consuming, a dead weight. Alcohol soon became my companion and by now, I had a very short fuse. I would have shot anyone who might have put a foot wrong.

Guard duty at the UN headquarters took me to in Nicosia. In a formal ceremony, we took over from The Black Watch Regiment. Thus, began two weeks of spit-and-polish and saluting anything that moved. After an extensive period of dining in the mountains on wild rabbits, rationed by the Brits, real food with chips at every meal and a half litre of milk a day was heaven. Some of the old sweats succumbed to the temptation of the red-light districts. With nothing to lose, I tagged along, on one occasion and presented myself to a pleasant lady in one of the dimly-lit brothels. In a bedroom, she undressed me and waited. It didn't take her long to realise that there would be no arousal. She kissed me on the forehead and told me to get dressed. When I offered her payment she politely and kindly refused. I returned to Limnitis and tried to bury the memory, downing glass after glass of Cyprus brandy during a session in the canteen.

Next morning, I couldn't be woken for guard duty. A medical officer was sent for and he brought me back from oblivion. A dull headache lingered for days and the realisation slowly dawned that the 'cure' that I had sought for the pain I carried had failed to work.

Somehow, probably through the banter among comrades, the military routine, the collective will to maintain law and order and preserve life in the chaotic world of slaughter around us, I made it through duties. The Greek soldiers celebrated when Dublin's Nelson's Pillar was blown up by the IRA. We couldn't care less. We joked about this tedious job, making light of the danger all around us. But I am certain that our presence saved many lives. By virtue of some invisible wall of protection – maybe even respect, or maybe they just liked us – both sides submitted to our presence and peace was maintained.

My next tour of duty began in the autumn – again in Cyprus – and I spent my twentieth birthday at a cold, wet and lonely observation post in Limnitis. The camp conditions had improved; the British engineers had built toilets and showers and the accommodation had been upgraded to four-man tents. Even our uniforms were now of a better quality, especially our rain gear. Within easy reach of Jerusalem, I found my thoughts wandering back, fearful yet curious. I decided to pay a return visit, perhaps hoping that by going back to the scene of the crime I could dispel the black dog of depression that lurked just under the surface. Something of the city must have impressed itself during those surreal, doom-laden days following the assault as I wandered aimlessly around the streets. This time I experienced a fleeting sense of the sacred that touched some part of me beneath the damaged shell that I now inhabited. I loved the old city. Some friends and I visited the Dome of the Rock, the second holiest place in the Muslim world. Inside, it was magnificent. Before entering the shrine, we had to remove our shoes and men with camel sticks stood, ready to beat anyone who attempted to enter without being suitably dressed. We stood at the

Wailing Wall, walked by the Jordan River, went to visit the tomb of Lazarus and the Dead Sea and prayed in the Church of the Nativity in Bethlehem, the place where Christ was born.

When I returned from Jerusalem, I found that we were stationed in Kokkina, several kilometres east of the Northern Cyprus mainland, surrounded by mountainous territory, with Morphou Bay on its northern flank. The bay looked inviting, but swimming was deemed to be too dangerous on account of fighting in the area. In August 1964, the Turkish Resistance paramilitary organisation (TMT), had landed arms and provisions from Turkey. The Greek Cypriot Nationalist Guerrilla Organisation (EOKA) retaliated by attacking the town on August the 6th, 1964. Four days later, Turkey sent in fighter jets to strafe and napalm villages and towns, causing heavy casualties. The UN intervened, preventing all-out war. But tensions were still high, and we could not afford to take any chances.

I welcomed the tension because any down time brought no respite from my own internal war; I had to be occupied. I had been drawing and sketching since I was a child. I particularly liked to draw cartoons and I began doodling again, using markers, pencils, pens – whatever was to hand. I was rather chuffed when I was asked to contribute to 'McAuley's Roundup', the A-Company news sheet. Based, as the name suggested on life on a ranch, the 'Roundup' was edited by Corporal Michael Lacy, aided and abetted by Signalman, John Durcan, Corporal Benny Molloy and myself. It made fun of all ranks from the CO down. Sending up one's colleagues, including the boss was a risky business so to protect ourselves, we used pseudonyms. Interest grew exponentially when the 'Roundup' featured in the third edition of *The Blue Beret,* in February 1966, a magazine that was issued by the information office of the United Nations Force in Cyprus. One man was curious to know who a certain character was based on, probably suspecting that it was based on him! It provided me with a pleasant distraction. Camp duties gave me something to fill working hours. For much of the time I assisted the cook, essentially boiling water for the tea on petrol-powered hydro cookers which were dangerous contraptions, to say the least. Water was not the only thing that boiled; I had broken out in boils and the medics concluded that the cause had been an over-abundance of iron in my blood, from eating too many eggs, supplied by the locals. Then, just prior to repatriation I developed a raging fever and I was taken to the Austrian field hospital where I was diagnosed with pneumonia and pleurisy. I was put in a wheelchair and wrapped in bed sheets that had been soaked in cold water in an effort to reduce my temperature. I shivered and sweated for three or four days with nurses taking my temperature at regular intervals. Finally, a driver showed up. "Get dressed," he said. "You're going home". The Austrian medical team were worried, but they were in no position to protest. I was given a massive shot of Penicillin and handed release papers to sign and I was on my way back to my unit. I could hardly breathe.

Wrapped in an army greatcoat, I arrived in Dublin where I was met by an ambulance and whisked to St. Bricin's Hospital. The course of Penicillin was continued and after a few days my buttocks were raw from needle punctures. An NCO with whom I had served in the Congo was admitted following a heart attack and placed in the next bed. I grew agitated listening to him trying to breathe. The doctor gave me sleeping tablets which had no effect and finally I heard his last breath. Three hours passed before his body was removed. Although I had been in a war zone, this was my first encounter with physical death up close – made all the more shocking by the fact that I knew the man personally, a man in the prime of life. I survived. The medical officer at St. Bricin's told me that I was cured and that if I wished I could return to Cyprus with the next unit.

I had become addicted to overseas duty and once again I volunteered. But on the flight to Nicosia I was having second thoughts.

I wanted to reinvent myself – somehow. I had left school before my sixteenth birthday, a lifetime ago. I had never worked in the world outside the army, apart from part-time stints in a bicycle shop, in the *Irish Times* and in Cassidy's. But I was an innocent and carefree schoolboy then. Now I was half a person, afraid that with one slip, my loathsomeness and defilement would be seen. My qualifications were confined to weaponry and military operations – in the lower ranks. I was a foot soldier, now sullied by the cold, calculating actions of a cowardly degenerate. All I had to show for my trouble was a little extra money and a few medals. The money was my only incentive to return to Cyprus.

At home, my father had a family friend whose daughter was considered to be an ideal 'catch'. On my next visit home, we were introduced. I was invited to meet her family. I put a slide-show of photographs together for them and it went well. We dated for a short while and we exchanged letters while I was overseas but when we next met, I had too much to drink. She was not impressed, and the relationship fizzled out.

CHAPTER 4

An Administrative Pain in the Backside

After the Anglo-Irish Treaty in December 1921, Ireland was a country divided. In 1922, fighting broke out between 'Free-Staters' and anti-Treaty forces and the ensuing Irish Civil War in the south of the island lasted less than a year but left lasting bitterness between political parties and families south of the border and between Catholics and Protestants in the north where Catholic Nationalists wished to see the whole island of Ireland united under the Irish flag and Protestant Unionists were supporters of the link with Britain. By and large, Catholics in Northern Ireland were the underclass, suffering discrimination in almost every area of life. I had served in war zones overseas. Now, just a hundred miles up the road, another simmering conflict was about to erupt.

Civil Rights marches began in the late 1960s, mainly through the city of Derry but soon, the marches became less about civil rights and more oriented towards Irish Republicanism. The paramilitary Irish Republican Army (IRA) joined in the peaceful protests. But in August 1969, large numbers of Catholics began a riot in Derry and the Royal Ulster Constabulary (RUC) tried to break them up in a fight that lasted for three days. It became known as the 'Battle of the Bogside'. In Belfast, entire streets of houses were burned down by Protestant rioters and over three thousand families, mainly Catholics, were driven from their homes. When the rioters began to use firearms, seven people were killed and a hundred were wounded.

South of the border, economic prosperity had shoved the issue of re-unification of the island off the political agenda and most people in the Republic were indifferent to the troubles in Northern Ireland. After six years' service I had left the Permanent Defence Forces and despite my fears, I decided to try my luck in civilian life. Aer Lingus, the national airline was recruiting loaders at Dublin Airport for the summer season. I joined a team of college students on the windy tarmac, loading and unloading baggage, sometimes amid the detritus of the aircraft toilets that was whipped about by the wind. Among the contents of the hold, steel coffins in transit, bound for repatriation and burial to other destinations were a grim reminder of the Vietnam War, still raging in South East Asia. But it was a tragic accident that brought a young Irish soldier home from Cyprus. Trooper Michael Kennedy died on July 1st, 1969 in a swimming pool accident and his remains were received with military honours at Dublin Airport. I met some of my old army friends who were in the guard of honour and as I watched the cortege move away, I suddenly felt adrift. I wanted to be back with my comrades in uniform.

The summer months passed quickly, and the end of my seasonal job forced me to find work elsewhere. I presented myself to another semi-state organisation, the Department of Posts and Telegraphs to seek employment as a trainee postman, working out of the Sheriff Street Post Office. Delivering post seemed a simple enough operation but I soon found that the strap of the heavy postbag slipped from my shoulder more often than it stayed on and the bag battered against my legs as I tried to maintain equilibrium on my trek from door to door. I probably would have overcome this by inventing some type of harness from one shoulder to the other except that, in order to become a permanent member of staff I would have to undergo an exam and an interview. This threw up another obstacle, a mandatory oral Irish exam involving a conversation in Gaelic, about 'Neidín', a school textbook story that was perhaps pertinent to my role – a story about a donkey!

As the situation in Northern Ireland began to look like it was descending into civil war, the Taoiseach, Jack Lynch said that the Irish government would not stand by and see innocent people injured. Some Unionists saw this as a threat by the government of the Republic to invade Northern Ireland. The UK government, realising that the Royal Ulster Constabulary (RUC), the North's police force, was not large enough to maintain law and order, sent the British Army into the cities of Belfast and Derry to support the RUC. Their presence, along with the violence that had erupted against Catholics gave new life to the IRA's eagerness to continue the campaign for a united Ireland. Some of the IRA members supported a non-violent policy while others accused the leadership of 'going soft'. This faction split from the IRA and formed the Provisional IRA, and a merciless bombing campaign began throughout Northern Ireland as well as on the British mainland. The Provisionals also targeted policemen and they became more and more involved in civilian demonstrations and riots. In retaliation, the loyalist Ulster Volunteer Force (UVF) began to use violence to protect the Protestant community from the Provisional IRA and launched their own offensives against Catholics – and against the Irish Republic. By August 1971, Internment (to arrest and hold people without charge) was introduced but internment intensified support for terrorism on both sides. On Sunday, the 30th of January 1972 a huge anti-Internment rally was organised in Derry. The march passed off peacefully but as the crowds disbanded, rioting broke out. British soldiers opened fire on the protestors and killed fourteen people, and 'Bloody Sunday' or 'The Derry Massacre' joined the long list of atrocities committed during 'The Troubles' in Northern Ireland.

The ongoing violence affected the whole of the Irish State as well as Great Britain and Northern Ireland. Bombings occurred in the border towns of Monaghan, Belturbet, Castleblayney, Clones and Dundalk resulting in death and injury in the Republic. Bombs exploding in Dublin and again in Monaghan, in 1973 resulted in horrific carnage and killings on the southern side of the border included those of high-profile figures such as Christopher Ewart Biggs, the British Ambassador to Ireland in 1976 and Lord Louis Mountbatten in Sligo in 1979.

With the escalation of the Troubles, Irish troops and Reserves were deployed along the border to provide assistance and protection to An Gárda Síochána – the unarmed civil police force in the Republic – as well as protection for the hundreds of refugees from Northern Ireland who were flooding into the border counties. Three new infantry battalions, the 27th the 28th and the 29th were established and the 4th Cavalry Squadron was redeployed to the border. The Irish Defence Forces purchased a new transport fleet, equipped soldiers with modern weapons and recruitment was stepped up.

I decided to re-enlist. I wanted to go to Artillery but was told that I would have to re-train as a recruit. Although I considered this a stupid policy, I went to the Curragh. It looked even more like a kip than I remembered! I immediately went 'AWOL', but the recruiting NCO telephoned me. "Go back to the Curragh, they'll be generous with you," he said. I followed his advice and returned the next day and was introduced to Sergeant O'Shea who was indeed generous and a rock of sense, a beacon of light in a dark place. He gave me a travel warrant and instructed me to go to Collins Barracks, Dublin. But on arrival there, I immediately applied for a "Discharge by Purchase". The Adjutant sent for me and gave me a severe bollocking; I had wanted to re-enlist, now I wanted to leave. I was an administrative pain in the backside. My desire to re-enlist eventually won out and I was armed with a sub-machine gun and given a job on guard duty on the back gate. After a few weeks, Commandant Andy Maguire came ambling up the hill and spoke to me. He was on full-time service, having been called up due to the Northern crisis. He had heard about my enlist/re-enlist shenanigans and he had something to tell me. "There's an education course pilot scheme commencing. I think you should apply", he said. "You can be studying for the Leaving Certificate examination at night while carrying out your army duties by day." I took his advice and went for it because I would be busy, with no time to ruminate. Shortly after this conversation I was asked if I would do border duty. I was delighted as it meant I would be occupied during the long, summer school holidays. My company commander said that the border posting would also bring a promotion to Acting Sergeant.

I was posted to Dundalk, an old garrison town close to the border and the last stop on the Republic side of the border on the Dublin-to-Belfast railway line. Following Partition in 1922, the Irish Free State had opened customs and immigration facilities at Dundalk to check goods and passengers crossing the border by train. The Irish Civil War of 1922–23 had seen a number of confrontations in Dundalk, one of which involved the local Fourth Northern Division of the old Irish Republican Army, the Anti-Treaty forces under Frank Aiken. They took over Dundalk barracks after the British left, but they were rounded up and detained by the National Army, the pro-treaty force in August 1922. A raid on Dundalk Jail freed Aiken and other anti-Treaty prisoners and two weeks later Aiken again took Dundalk Barracks and captured its garrison. Instead of holding the town however, he called for a meeting in the centre of town to garner a truce. Aiken was later a founding member of the Fianna Fáil party. He was first elected to Dáil Éireann in 1923 and was re-elected at each subsequent election until 1973. He held several ministerial posts including Minister for Defence. As Minister for External Affairs, he delivered a speech on nuclear disarmament to the UN General Assembly in October 1958 and accompanied John F. Kennedy on his official Irish tour in 1963. It was under Aiken's watch that the first Irish UN peacekeeping mission was mounted in 1960 and Aiken had visited the Irish troops during that first mission in the Congo. Dundalk

Barracks was renamed Aiken Barracks in 1986 after Frank Aiken.

Nicknamed 'El Paso', after the Texan town on the border with Mexico, the town of Dundalk's position close to the border with Northern Ireland was rumoured to harbour a 'nest' of IRA activists during the Troubles. I found it dull and dreary with a gloomy atmosphere that seemed to weigh me down. The company commander in Dundalk knew me from my time training recruits in Cathal Brugha Barracks. He said that he couldn't promote me because I was not a 'specialist', meaning that I was not qualified to instruct in mortars or machine guns. I was however wont to dispense advice to others as to how to work on their career trajectories. One young soldier found himself at the receiving end of a treatise on promotion while occupying a top bunk bed in Dundalk Barracks. I am not sure if it was my advice or his ambition that worked for him, but he went on to become the youngest sergeant major in the Irish Defence Forces.

The commanding officer, a gruff Antrim man and a real soldier, suggested that I transfer to Castleblayney. I agreed, knowing that some of my friends from Collins Barracks were already stationed there. There was seldom a newspaper that didn't carry a story about the troubles in the North and I was half expecting Cyprus again – with perhaps more sophisticated accommodation and amenities. But duties consisted mainly of patrols and guard duty. I had taken up running and the countryside around Castleblayney provided some pleasant and varied terrain for an early morning run. The forces of the British Crown that were north of the border seemed to have matters under control and there were no terrorist incidences in our neck of the woods. We mixed with the locals and if there were any IRA or Loyalist sympathisers among them, they didn't make themselves known – overtly or covertly. The Ponderosa Public House had Country and Western music on offer and it became our watering hole. The only threat to our well-being was the possibility of an ambush on our way back to base by local lads who took exception to local girls taking up with soldiers whose spending power was viewed as a lethal attraction! I missed out on promotion, but I had some good fun.

Back in Dublin, I applied myself to study with gusto and passed my Leaving Cert. exams and was then encouraged to attend university. In 1973 I registered in the Faculty of Commerce at University College Dublin for a four-year degree course, again studying at night, taking a bus into the centre of the city and another bus out to the university campus in Donnybrook on the south side. First year was murder: lectures on five nights a week and a tutorial on Saturday. I took extra tuition at Leeson Street College during Easter, to brush up on my Maths. I failed two subjects in the summer exams but passed them in winter – a hard lesson. Second year in college was a doddle in comparison to the graft of first year. There was no exam in year three, just case studies and essays – fourteen essays and four case studies. In year four I did Management Accounting, Financial Accounting, Business Systems, Marco Economics, the National Economics of Ireland, and Finance. I graduated in 1977 and was selected to undergo a one-year course in the Curragh for a Commission. This was a big surprise as I had never sought a commission. It was also a great boost to my morale.

I met a school teacher from the Midlands, a very attractive girl with red hair and blue eyes, and we went began to date. After many long afternoons chatting and 'snogging' in the Phoenix Park, we decided to go away to Donegal for a 'dirty weekend'. The 'dirty weekend' didn't materialise, however. I had the same difficulty that I had in the brothel in Nicosia. I was deeply embarrassed and ashamed. This time, my lady friend wrote me a 'Dear John' letter. When our relationship ended, I lost interest in sex. The prospect of relating on a romantic level had become quite frightening. My stealthily approaching thirties looked like old age and with it, the fading hope of ever settling down and having a family of my own. I was scared about the future.

Work kept me going. I managed to secure a position in Eastern Area Records in the Adjutant General's Branch, documenting the 43rd Battalion who were about to travel overseas. I handled Garda clearances and promotions, and all documents requiring signature were brought to me to be checked before being passed on to the Officer-in-Charge for his signature. It was just what I needed, although it was tedious, painstaking work for staff who had to hand-notate soldiers' individual records. John Egan, later to become Sergeant Major in 'A' Administration, looked after Discharges. John was particularly helpful to me as regards the work and during lunch-time, we played badminton which provided a welcome break as well as an opportunity have a bit of exercise and a bit of fun. Staff member, David Pentony was also full of fun and an absolute joy to work with. News of his untimely death in a road traffic accident came as a shocking blow that was felt by everyone, without exception. It was the second time I had lost someone I knew, albeit at some remove. Thankfully I had not witnessed the accident, but the suddenness of his death affected me nonetheless. For the first time in months, I could feel the dark cloud descend around me but as things began to return to normal after David's death, I was lifted up again.

With a college degree under my belt, I was selected for commissioning in 1978 and travelled to the Military College at the Curragh in November to begin the 4th Potential Officers' Course, looking forward to a new chapter but sad to leave my colleagues behind. At the Curragh I was met by the smell of turf smoke and the twenty-four others who would be in my class. Training and classes began the following day – in Recruit Training, Junior Leader training, and NCO training. We had square training, drilled by a corporal. The tactics were enjoyable: Offence, Defence and Retrograde Operations. We did a night shoot and attack during two weeks' training back in the Glen of Imaal. We did a course in the Army School of Administration on Quartermastering and Adjunting as well as a sub-catering course at the Army School of Catering.

We studied Transportation, did Syndicates on Geophysical Studies and studied History and Military Symbols. Later on, we had Sword Drill. Extra-curricular activities included soccer which we played indoors in bad weather. I had inherited a liking for the game from my father but although I was nifty and fast. I never excelled at it and got into trouble many a time. I almost had my leg broken during an indoor soccer game by a fellow who must have thought we were playing in a World Cup game.

I finished the course in 6th place out of twenty-five and I became a commissioned officer on the 1st of November 1979. In February 1980, my report from the colonel of the Military College stated that I was an excellent student, with highly commendable work, that I had a pleasant and modest personality, good powers of reasoning, great resilience in field exercises, a shrewd, tactical brain and that I should make an excellent officer. But I did not see the report. Class reports are passed on to the office of the Chief of Staff where they remain on file, gathering dust. I never knew until many years later what my report contained. I considered myself very fortunate to have made it to the college because in those days the process involved a recommendation from one's commanding officer followed by two interviews. Looking back, I wonder if my report would have made any difference to my self-esteem. I wonder too how I could possibly have had 'a pleasant and modest personality' and a 'shrewd, tactical brain' while trying to keep depression at bay. I can only conclude that I was so engrossed in the packed curriculum that I had no time to ruminate.

At the end of November, I was posted to the far end of the country, to the 1st Motor Squadron in Fitzgerald Camp, Fermoy in County Cork. The barracks was a former British Army base that had been used for training troops for service in India. The town of Fermoy expanded around these facilities and retained its British military facilities until 1922 when the Irish Free State was first established. During the War of Independence, Fermoy was the scene of the first attack by the IRA against British troops and following the Treaty of 1921 and the subsequent Irish Civil War, the town had suffered badly, and most buildings were dilapidated. A nearby aerodrome which had been owned by Britain's Royal Flying Corps (RFC) was handed over the Irish Air Corps in 1923. The downtown area of Fermoy was built on a flood plain that straddled the River Blackwater which was prone to serious flooding. Whenever the town flooded, the army would be called in to ferry residents across the submerged bridge to the north of the town and safety. The area further up along the Blackwater was one of scenic beauty, especially in autumn when the road to Tallow and Lismore was resplendent in autumn gold.

My fellow officers were all Dubliners, like myself, with the exception of the officer commanding and three captains who hailed from Cork, Cobh, Blackpool and Glanworth, respectively. The officer commanding was Commandant Tom Stapleton, a gentle giant. He was standing in for another commandant who was on overseas duty. I was Quartermaster in charge of Ordnance, Food Bedding, Clothing, Fuel, Light, Accommodation, Lands, Cooks, Dining, Rations and Staff. On arrival, I had to do a full audit of all accounts. The ordnance account was in order, but I found deficiencies in Rations and Clothing. When I reported this to Comdt. Stapleton, he ordered two senior quartermasters from the 13th Battalion to do a re-check and two NCO quartermasters confirmed my findings. There were forty-two combat jackets short. We were close to Kilworth firing ranges and cavalry officers would ask the quartermaster for a loan of a combat jacket, which would never again see the inside of Fitzgerald Camp. The commandant followed up with calls to his friends and within three months all was in order – just in time for a Quartermaster General's inspection. What the inspector didn't know was that we had borrowed clothing from Depot Ordnance in Cork by virtue of a 'temporary voucher'. The items could be returned to Cork when no longer required. But my

Catholic scruples would not allow me to sign the voucher.

Other issues arose with my boss, now returned from overseas. I wanted to run a tightly organised and transparent accounting system and his nonchalance annoyed me intensely. One evening, I wanted to check the contents of a freezer store room. The corporal on duty informed me that the keys were locked away. "Get them or I'll shoot the lock off!" I told him. The keys were produced. Any speck of sparkle from my shiny, new officer status and any shred of self-esteem I had remaining after the pain and humiliation of Jerusalem abruptly disappeared after a stag party for one of the officers. After a few drinks in the pub we came back to the officers' mess where the poor groom-to-be was chained to the bar and the drinking began in earnest. He was soon released but not before he had to perform a rendition of the Ray Charles hit, 'Take These Chains from My Heart'. On my way to bed, I was passing by a room occupied by another fellow officer. The door was open, and he was sprawled on his bed, hands behind his head. "Goodnight", I said. "Yeah, a good night, wasn't it?" he said. We chatted about the evening and had a few laughs, both bleary-eyed. As I got up to leave, he mumbled, "By the way, there's a rumour going around that you're gay." The fog of inebriation evaporated. "Where did you hear that?" I asked him. "Tom said it – after you guys came back from Greece."

Tom was twenty-three, a tall, handsome footballer with legs like tree-trunks, who drew women to him like moths to a flame. He was also a sun-worshipper who liked to show off his designer t-shirts against a year-round suntan. Bored, I had agreed to accompany him on a short package holiday to Greece. A break in the sun seemed like a good idea and I wanted to see the sights in Paros and especially in Athens. We were barely airborne when I was having second thoughts. Lying on a beach in the sun would be the most boring thing imaginable. But as it happened, Tom was interested in Greece's cultural and historical past and we spent an enjoyable couple of days taking it all in. By night, Tom's interests favoured the nightclubs and the female 'talent'. I was preoccupied – agitated and annoyed, berating myself for having left my camera in the boot of a taxi on the way to the hotel and despite subsequent enquiries to the taxi company, it was never found. I had bought the camera in the Congo and had treasured it and I was heartbroken. A few drinks seemed like a good idea to take the edge off my agitation, but I had a few too many and soon, the bar was swimming in and out of focus. Unlike the session in Cyprus however, on this occasion I vomited my guts out and remained compos mentis.

My foreboding on the way to Greece had become a self-fulfilling prophecy. I also contracted some sort of stomach bug and I spent our last day afraid to venture too far away from the toilets. At the airport our flight back to Dublin was delayed and then cancelled. As we waited for another flight I immediately booked a room back at the hotel for one more night. Tom had other ideas. He met a young lady who was travelling to Dublin and discovered that there was one seat available on the same flight. Off they went, and I returned to the hotel. Tom had concluded that I didn't appear to be a ladies' man. In his mind there must have been only one reason for that. But I liked Tom. For all his posing he was cultured, intelligent and good fun. Maybe I was jealous of him too. I thought I looked and acted like everyone else. Inside I was broken, sure of only one thing: I must stay in the army, go through the motions and act like a soldier – at least for the time being. But my inability to envisage any sort of personal relationship or any sort of future seemed to be getting worse.

It is only in retrospect that I can see the beginnings of my downward spiral in the army. I was inflexible and unreasonable, hung up on scruples, obsessive about the letter of the law and on rules and regulations, without the ability to deal with anyone unless they were on my wavelength. I was prone to knee-jerk reactions, always on the alert for anything out of place and unrelenting in the pursuit of wrongdoing, as I saw it. If I found wrongdoing, I wanted heads to roll. It would take a long time to join the dots between all of this and what was really going on beneath the surface.

But in the early days, before all of this, there had been some who had seen something in me that must have impressed them. One of these was none other than the Chief of Staff of the Defence Forces, Lieutenant General Louis Hogan. A dinner in the Officers' Mess in Kilworth was coming up, with the generals and senior civil servants were catered for a smaller room. The catering went very well. The officers in Limerick sent a case of wine for the VIP. Our Transport Sergeant, 'Flappy' Hogan was offered the first bottle and we handed over the rest to the colonels' table. After dinner, the VIPs came into the kitchen to thank the cooks. I was introduced to the Chief of Staff. "Ah, sure I know him well," Lt. Gen. Hogan said. "Didn't I train him?" Years earlier he had been President of the Central Interview Board that had recommended me for commissioning. He knew me well by that time because I had helped him deliver meals-on-wheels around Dublin.

CHAPTER 5

Facing Death in a Wadi

The Peacekeeper guards his post
Observing the past.
The same ground of ancient wars
his No-Man's Land.

No Man's Land, Michael J. Whelan

In the fourteen years since I had visited Lebanon, first as a peace-keeper, a broken teenage soldier and later passing through as a pil-grim tourist searching for answers, the country had descended into chaos. From 1978, a battalion of Irish troops had been deployed as part of the United Nations Interim Force (UNIFIL) in Lebanon. The Irish troops were initially intended to supervise the withdrawal of the Israeli Defence Forces (IDF) from the area after an invasion in 1978 and prevent fighting between the Palestine Liberation Orga-nization (PLO) forces and Israel. I joined the newest battalion in April 1980. The nightmares of Jerusalem persisted but I carried out my duties and as far as I knew, I appeared to be normal – on the surface. I had completed a driving course in the School of Motoring at the Curragh Camp. This was to benefit me when I applied and was selected to go to Lebanon as an officer. But, I was having second thoughts and wanted to withdraw my application. I might have been an administrative pain in the backside again, but for the At Tiri incident.

On April 18th shortly before our deployment, Private Derek Smallhorne and Private Thomas Barrett were on a UN Peacekeep-ing patrol in South Lebanon when the patrol was ambushed by the

Pro-Israeli Militia Grouping, near a place called At Tiri. The ambushers killed Private Smallhorne, a thirty-one-year-old a father of three, and Private Barrett, aged twenty-nine, father of a baby daughter. They tortured and shot a third Irishman, Private John O'Mahony and kidnapped Steve Hindy, a former Middle East correspondent for the Associated Press, who happened to be with the Irishmen when the ambush took place. Hindy and Private O'Mahony were the only two who survived what became known as 'the At Tiri Incident'. The At Tiri Incident changed my mind. If I withdrew my application I would have been deemed a coward. I was also gaining skills, experience and rising in the ranks and my section in Fermoy were outstanding professionals. We cared for each other and it was this connection with them that, after some hesitation, influenced my decision to go with them.

My commanding officer was Freddie Swords, whose training was very exact and intensive. He gave me the nickname, 'Roger' because I replied to every instruction with, "Roger" or "Roger, Sir". Training over, the 47th Battalion formed up in Kilworth and we were on our way. When we arrived in Beirut we were collected by truck and driven to our post. Danger was palpable in the air and we were on high alert at all times. Our company, B Company, was deployed to As-Sultaniyah as the reserve – two up and one in the rear: standard dispositions – with responsibility for Tibnin Bridge. My section comprised three Panhard AML90s and two armoured personnel carriers (APCs). I was the Recce Section Commander in B Company, 47th Bn, and 2 i/c Support Platoon. The At Tiri incident at Easter was at the forefront of our minds for much of the time. To my mind, the decision to send three drivers into the 'Enclave' was stupid, as was the decision the following year to post two young soldiers, Hugh Doherty and Kevin Joyce without an NCO on the reserve slope of a wadi in Deir Ntar, a place that lives in my memory – for another, more personal reason.

B Coy, 47th Bn. was based in As Sultaniyah, the Bn reserve. Two other companies were in Barashit and Haddatha. Sultaniyah had Deir Ntar and Tibnin Bridge to control and Barashit had Bayt Yahoun – 'the Black Hole'. The Black Hole was a static checkpoint. Bayt Yahoun was in a class of its own. An AML 90 and crew manned this post 24/7, facing into the DFF compound with its Sherman tank. It also had an APC parked there to prevent vehicular incursions by the DFF. Tibnin Bridge was a crossroads of critical importance – three roads leading to As Sultaniyah, Deir Ntar, Barashit and Tibnin town. Haddatha had Hill 880 and the road to At Tiri – a very valuable asset.

In my first location I was tasked with Company OPS duties – canteen administration and the occasional patrol. Eventually, we were rotated to Barashit where reconnaissance was added to my portfolio. One day I took an armoured vehicle to Tibnin with Cpl. Tagdh Daly, an excellent driver. Then the shit hit the fan. The Israelis said that if the armoured vehicle didn't get off the track, they would blow it off. When we returned to base, everyone was wearing flak jackets. My boss, Freddie Swords came and shook my hand – delighted because the IDF used to say that the Irish did no patrolling! In hindsight it was a stupid thing to do. We could have hit a landmine anywhere along that road. I also took chances going over Hill 880 at Tiri at night to give the crew a canteen break. Cpl Tagdh Daly could drive up Hill 880, changing the gears from 'Road' to 'Cross-Country' without taking a breath. There was a static AML 90 there, facing the IDF's 'Brown Mound' and we were always in their sights as they watched our every move.

I was proud of my section. The Company Reserve was comprised of APCs and infantry. I was tasked with this also. We had one major scare when Post 880 was attacked. In response, one of our younger soldiers – a boy from Kilkenny – 'warmed the wadi' with gunfire and my boss was very impressed with him. And yet lots of young soldiers were scared. This was a worry for officers. I discussed it with my boss who agreed that as much as sixty percent of our Company could not be trusted when their security was threatened. When my section was employed as Infantry, the members resented it. I took their complaint to Comdt. Swords but as he had lost operational control by that time and he could do nothing.

To supplement food rations, our resourceful cook, Corporal Flynn would commandeer a jeep and take off in a cloud of dust with a consignment of whiskey on board and reappear after a day or two with fresh food. Water was a scarce resource, but we had a water truck which would fill tanks in Company areas on a rota system. The water truck drivers were very brave, each journey could mean danger and to minimise their exposure, water was rationed. Showers were infrequent. My heart went out to the soldiers, their backs salt-encrusted from their webbing and their lips dry and cracked, who lived under canvas while the officers – of which I was one – were fortunate to be accommodated in a house and shelter from the searing desert heat.

Tragedy struck when a large boulder fell onto an armoured vehicle and Sergeant Ted Yates, who was a passenger was killed. The driver had lost control of the steering wheel and the car rode up along a bank and overturned. Ted was the only casualty. The mood of the camp changed from the usual light-hearted banter to shock, then mourning. For Ted's commanding officer, Gerry Cooney, it was especially difficult having to convey the awful news to the sergeant's family back home. The chaplain offered a Mass for Ted and his family and I wondered what consolation prayer would bring to those who mourned him. By now, religion was beginning to hold little if any comfort for me. I had slowly become disillusioned with all of it. I was beginning not to care whether or not I lived. But in just over twenty-four hours this ambivalence would be put to the test.

On July 1st, 1980 I was leading a four-man night patrol, with a junior NCO and three privates, along a wadi near Deir Ntar Village. The air was heavy with the scent of trees. Overhead, clouds raced across a bright moon, casting dark shadows one minute, illuminating the landscape the next. The sound of Mullahs, singing prayers – "God is Great" in Arabic – was reassuring. Our patrol was about twenty minutes out from our platoon post, 'Loc.-622', picking our way through rough terrain when I noticed that two privates were not up with the rest of the party. I posted the remaining private as rear security, and my corporal and I went back to see what had happened to the two missing men. *At Tiri again? Had they been kidnapped?* After about ten minutes I found one of them sitting on a sloping bank under a gnarled tree and asked him if he was hurt. He looked unhurt, but I could feel my legs buckling and I began to think the worst. *Had this soldier been planted under the tree as a ruse to draw someone into a trap?* "Six twenty-three B. Six twenty-three B," he replied. He had a glazed look in his eyes and I realised that something was wrong. He was incoherent, high on something – probably cannabis.

I slowly removed the magazine from his FN rifle and handed the magazine to my corporal. Then somewhere off to my right I heard the click-clack of a bullet being released up the breech of a rifle. "You're in trouble, Sir," my corporal said. I turned and saw the second soldier stalking out of the shadows with his rifle cocked and pointed in my direction. "Don't take his weapon! Don't take his weapon!" he shouted. My mouth dried up and my throat was tightening. My legs felt like they would go from under me. But some form of survival instinct took over. I gripped my pistol, just to feel and hold onto something solid. "We're all friends here," I said. "Have a drink of water." Ever so slowly he dropped the rifle, barrel pointing to the ground and sat down. Then without being ordered, he said he was going to take out the round from the breech and apply the safety catch. I ordered the rest of the party to sit down and take up security positions and watched as he slowly removed the round. I then checked the other soldier's weapon. Adrenalin was pumping through me, sweat soaking my hair underneath my helmet which felt like a steel vice encircling my head. Immediately, depersonalisation struck, starting with the tingling tremor in my legs – the all too familiar scenario that I had suffered in Jerusalem. I could feel my heart racing and my breathing reduced to short gasps. In seconds, I would be in a crumpled heap on the ground, completely at the mercy of two individuals – two of our own soldiers – who were out of their heads. I could not believe that I had been attacked by my own comrades – first in Jerusalem and now in Lebanon. *Not again*! I thought. "We have reached our objective," I said through dried lips. "We will sit and observe for twenty minutes and then return." I radioed the base to inform them of our plan and waited for things to cool down. After some time, we got to our feet and headed back to the platoon post. The aggressor was holding firmly onto his weapon and clearly had no intention of handing it over to anyone. He then offered to carry the radio set and I allowed him to do this as we made our way back to base. When we arrived at Loc. 6-22 I instructed the party to take off their equipment and relax. All the weapons were put to one side and I asked the guard commander to call for medical help for the two drugged soldiers. "They are both in a bad condition and appear to have heat stroke," I said. I quietly told a guard to lock away their weapons and if either of the two made a false move that he was to shoot them! All I could think of was revenge.

I rang Commandant Swords and briefed him on the situation and advised him that the pair were not allowed near weapons on their return to camp. Two officers and the Medical NCO arrived with an escort. The medics looked at the pair, swaying about, faces red as tomatoes and told them to go outside and wash themselves down. Heatstroke was a ruse, but it worked. The two soldiers were brought under escort to Tibnin Hospital. I had managed to hold myself together but in the weeks that followed, nightmares returned with a vengeance. Daylight hours brought no respite from panic attack after panic attack. Anger tormented me but there was nowhere and no way to vent. It was not until too many years later that I found out that the change in me had been observed and noted. In a confidential staff report, dated the 26th of February 1993, my Commanding Officer, Commandant Freddie Swords stated that before the incident I had been well adjusted, good humoured and that I had integrated well with all ranks. On occasions after the incident it was noted that I 'revealed a degree of moodiness and introversion which was unusual and uncharacteristic'.

In my left pocket in the wadi in South Lebanon on 1st of July 1980 I had a relic given to me by a lady in Drogheda. It had a small cross and an image of the Virgin Mary on one side and a picture of Pope John Paul II on the other. When I saw it, I was inclined to attribute my survival of that incident to him, a canonised saint, chosen by God for whom time has no meaning and nothing is impossible. If it wasn't him, someone else in the higher realms was looking out for me!

Commandant Swords had given me the use of his land rover while he was on leave in Cyprus. He was now going on leave and again offered me the use of a land rover. "Take it," he insisted, in response to my objections, "I want you to go around and check on things every day". It was a sign of his trust in me and I would never forget it. Days later, when he returned from leave, I came upon him and his second-in-command having a bite to eat. I had heard them arguing and they were both in foul mood and no longer talking to each other. Freddie was having a bowl of soup. At length he said, "So, Roger, what's been happening while I've been away?" "I had an erection, Sir," I said. Freddie's spoon shot out of his hand in a spray of soup. His second-in-command burst out laughing. I laughed at my own cynicism, all too agonisingly aware that such an event had as much likelihood of happening as a trip to Mars.

Back on duty, I was acting post commander in Bayt Yahoun, a flash point in South Lebanon. The security procedure was that the platoon officer and the platoon sergeant would rotate every twenty-four hours. I was 'resting off' in bed when I was awoken by raised voices. I heard someone shout, "Shut up, or I'll knife you!" I jumped out of bed and quickly dressed and slipped my pistol, suspended from my lanyard, into my right-hand pocket, still jumpy and anxious after the wadi incident. I stepped into the corridor and walked past the door of the room next to mine. The occupants, two sergeants, one nicknamed 'The Parrot', were arguing at the top of their voices. "Any tea?" I shouted to the cook as I pounded down the corridor. "No problem, Sir," the cook shouted back to me. The argument stopped. Had either of the sergeants stepped out or displayed any form of aggression in my presence, I would have shot him there and then!

In July 1980, after the incident in Deir Ntar, I was given leave time. I went to Nicosia only to find myself sliding into another black hole of depression and I knew I was having a breakdown. I phoned Jim O'Brien, the unit welfare officer, 47th Inf. He arranged for a flight through a local travel agent, who called to my hotel where with the tickets. Back in Lebanon I was travelling from the airport to the UN house in a taxi. Suddenly, the taxi screeched to a halt and three men jumped in. I almost passed out with fright. My first thought: *kidnap*! I would have chosen death rather than face captivity. Then, just as suddenly as they had jumped in, they jumped out again. Shaken, I asked the driver to drop me at a nearby UN post. I spent the night on an army cot, fighting off rising terror. The next day I heard that a ration truck was heading back to HQ. I asked the officer who was in charge if I could hitch a lift and was happy to sit in the back of the truck, among bags of potatoes all the way back to our area of operations. Freddie Swords was very glad to see me.

But there was no escape from danger. One evening a couple of high-end cars drove into our Post, flags flying. The second in command to Major Hadaad of the South Lebanese Army (SLA) had come to tell us calmly that the town of Ayta Az Zutt was about to be shelled. I was aware that the SLA referred to their commanding officer as 'Major'. I asked him if he would like to speak with our 'Major'. If I had said 'commanding officer' he would not have understood. He agreed and produced a box of Dutch cigars and offered it to me. "Would you like a coffee?" I asked. "Yes," he said. While we waited in the tent for the 'major' to arrive, he told me that "Forty-Six Battalion, LA Battery. Forty-Seven Battalion, Mingy Battery". 'Mingy' was a word that we acquired from our time in the Congo. It means 'many' or 'much'. He was clearly not impressed by the 46th Battalion but he was in no doubt that the SLA were not to mess with the 47th! When Freddie Swords, our 'major' arrived, the two talked for a few minutes and then our visitors left. Forty minutes later the shelling of Ayta Az Zutt began. All we could do was stand by and listen to the noise of the shelling, trying not to think about the carnage that was being deliberately and callously created amid the smoke and the fire – under our noses – a sickening, bloody mess that ambulance personnel and UN troops would have to clean up, to the accompaniment of sirens, the wailing survivors, the pitiful cries of orphaned children and the stench of charred and burning human and animal flesh. When it was all over I smoked the cigars until the box was empty.

In another incident, our rations vehicle was stopped and two of our soldiers were robbed of their rifles and held at gunpoint. I summoned a group of my men and I called a 'Cola boy' forward. He abandoned his little cart of Cola and came with me to the scene. He was just a kid, but he could speak French. The SLA spoke French as well as Arabic. Some could speak English but refused to engage with us in English. We approached the thieves who were preventing the jeep from moving. "Return the weapons," I said. They immediately pulled out a couple of grenades from their pockets to intimidate me. "I'll do a John Wayne," I told my men; meaning that I would dive to the ground and start shooting. They would have followed suit. The thieves must have understood. They released the men and returned their weapons.

An incident could erupt at any second, without warning and we were on alert at all times. Following an accidental shooting in a house in Haddatha, the roof and a wall collapsed onto a corporal's back. Fortunately, he survived. This constant state of volatility in our area, on top of all my personal issues was taking its toll. As I was driving an armoured personnel carrier from an operations post to Tibnin I accidentally dislocated the gear lever. I could only sit helplessly on the vehicle, trying to stave off a panic attack, mouth dry, unable to speak while a trooper did the repairs. I wasn't alone; a lot of soldiers were frightened. I had seen the fear in their eyes on a patrol to Hill 880. Frightened soldiers could be unpredictable and a danger to their officers. But knowing that others were affected was of little consolation to me; I was coming to the end of my tether. Something had to give.

Our battalion commander must have seen or sensed my agitation. He ordered me to take seventy-two hours' leave. I would accompany the battalion chaplain and our second-in-command who were going on a short break to, of all places, Jerusalem! I almost refused but I had to obey the order or be court martialled – or worse still, repatriated. Career over. We spent the next couple of days window shopping in Jerusalem and although I was with the chaplain, neither of us visited a shrine or set foot in a temple. I wrote postcards to my mother who made no secret of the fact that she always worried about me whenever I was overseas. But she was glad of the money from my 'credits' – money that was kept by for soldiers' next of kin in the event that they died while on overseas service. I bought Rosary beads and a Bible which I brought home for Grand-Aunt Bridget. Bridget, who often asked why I hadn't been to see her could never be told that I was in the army for fear that she too would be worried about me – until I arrived home with the beads and the Bible! The 'Jerusalem Bible' and the 'Holy Rosary Beads' made it all okay and I was pressed into long, tour guide descriptions of the Holy Land over tea and cake. Little did Bridget, or my mother know what Jerusalem really meant to me!

The leave time in Jerusalem did little for my condition. I was becoming short-tempered and aggressive and I slept with my pistol within reach. The Advance Party of the 48th Infantry Battalion would be arriving in a couple of weeks and we would be handing the Operational Control of our unit over to them. At this time our minds were more focused on going home, glad to be leaving before the weather would turn cold and rain came. Then I had an almighty row with Commandant Danny Flood, the incoming commanding officer when I brought a complaint to him about my troops now having to man static Infantry posts. They had complained bitterly to me and I agreed with them. In my opinion they had been through enough. But the CO was having none of it. His dismissal of the complaint was unexpected. I had known Danny in Cyprus and we all loved him. He was a good singer and he would bring the house down with 'There is Nothing Like a Dame'. On Day Two, he arrived at breakfast and was taken aback to find that all we had to eat was fried bread. Next day he brought a bottle of ketchup to garnish it. The officers ate the same food as the men which was good for morale and Danny had already ingratiated himself with the troops. But I didn't speak to him for the remaining two weeks.

As we approached the end of our mission, we had a visit from an RTE TV crew who were filming a programme about the Irish in Lebanon. We assembled outside Company Headquarters to select a member of the unit who had all the attributes desired by the crew to be a spokesperson – tall, handsome, sexy, tanned and a good speaker. The interview was to take place on Hill 880 with the MIO present. Commandant Freddie Swords had always emphasised the importance of maintaining our high standards of dress and deportment. I had taken this on board and vowed that I would make sure that the standards would be maintained. We arrived on the Hill-880 and the soldier who had been selected for interview was asked to remove his shirt. "This will not happen, but he may remove his cravat," I told the director who grudgingly accepted this compromise. Mike Murphy, the celebrity presenter with RTE, didn't get involved. After the interview, photographs were taken by the Stills Photographer with the crew and I was part of a patrol that accompanied Mike Murphy and his crew down a wadi. This wadi was dangerous at times – mainly at night and it was used by AEs travelling from one area to another. We were taking risks, but the cameraman and the photographer wanted more photographs. Later, I was detailed, together with Sgt. Joe Scott, to accompany the RTE crew to Beirut – unarmed. We stayed overnight in the Commodore Hotel where later in the evening, I bumped into Mike Murphy. He was very gracious and invited us to join the crew for dinner. Naturally, we attended.

But I was still bitter about my altercation with Danny Flood. This would be one of many instances of petty grievances that would eventually be my downfall. I managed to regain some strength after the wadi incident, but my mind was fractured. I was rewarded with an outbreak of shingles, which was very painful, especially on the journey home – on Chalk 3, the last Chalk, to leave. My mother had bought a new bed, and new bedclothes for me. I would have slept on a bed of nails, happy to be home. Had our tour of duty not ended I would have killed someone! On their return home from Lebanon both Frank Stewart and Freddie Swords submitted their reports in which they said that I displayed courage and outstanding leadership qualities during my tour of duty. But I did not have sight of these until after 1993 and I wonder if they would have changed any of the subsequent events of my life and career.

After some time on leave I was back in Fermoy to take up from where I had left off in April and I tried to put the wadi incident as far from my mind as possible. In the beginning I got along well with my boss. We would often run a circuit around the old Kilcrumper cemetery together and called ourselves, 'The Kilcrumper

Harriers'. But eventually we fell out over an army exercise that was held in Kilworth Training Camp. After the exercise, cavalry officers came to Fitzgerald Camp and a meal was arranged by the second officer in command. It was served in the dining hall with thick brown stew, the only item on the menu. Some of the officers complained to the boss that the stew was 'awful'. He immediately sent for the cook who had, by this time gone home and he had to report back to barracks to be subjected to an interrogation. I had been in the town and on my return was tipped off by the military policeman at the gate that the CO was 'on the warpath'. I walked down the corridor to the officers' mess. He was on the high stool at the bar with a friend form Cork. He invited me to join them for a drink. I declined. I asked to have a word with him in his office. "Commandant, you are up my nose," I said. "I am reporting you the Brigadier!" But the Brigadier was a friend of his and so nothing came of my complaint. I regret my actions, borne of naiveté and misguided scruples. My principles were unyielding. By then, I had morphed into an individual as far removed from the innocent, 'timid little bastard' as was possible to imagine. It was my way or no way. I was in pain but didn't know it and my days with the 1st Motor Squadron were numbered.

The 1st Motor Squadron was formed in 1939 and landed in Fermoy in 1948. It was the nucleus of the 4th and 5th Motor Squadrons that served in the Curragh, Kilkenny, Clonmel and Ballincollig. To be honest, it was a privilege to serve in this unit, an oasis of hospitality on the road to Cork. We had visitors who came to Fitzgerald Camp for petrol and a cuppa and when I look back at my three years there, I do so with fondness, and dare I say it, love. The 1st might be regarded by some as clannish but there was good in their hearts. They tolerated me, a novice and I was the better for it. I would gladly return to the 1st and the long conversations after dinner – and the running. We did a lot of that. I was part of the Southern Command Cross-Country team in 1982. I ran three marathons and several 'An Cosantóir' 10k team races.

I had also made some civilian friends in Fermoy, one of whom was interested in music. Some years later, we would attend the Bayreuther Festspiele in 1996, my first performance of *Parsifal*. Unfortunately, my friend became ill during Act 1 and had to leave the theatre. The following year we managed to get tickets again and this time there were no problems. Having someone who shared a love of music was a godsend. We talked endlessly, walked and played chess and on Saturdays we would have a few pints at The Hill Hotel and then drive over the mountain road to Fermoy or have lunch in Cloyne or at the Garryvoe Hotel, famous in Cork for Sunday lunch.

I was introduced to Ballycotton by a friend from Dublin who liked to go fishing there. I immediately fell in love with the village and stayed in the hotel. I brought my parents and my two aunts for a visit. My father loved the hotel, especially the ample amounts of toast that accompanied the Irish breakfast. There was a viewing area that was much sought after by people who had summer houses in the village, which meant that we had to be out early to get seats. On one Sunday, I put one of my aunts on sentry duty beside four seats. She was a big woman and a force to be reckoned with and despite some complaining from the summer house folks, she held her ground. I still love Ballycotton and I have longed to go back and spend some time there but until recently I had not been able to face the memories of happier times there with my family, my father in particular. But, as I write, I have a new memory – of taking a good friend and his wife up on a long-standing invitation to visit.

The whole area around Fermoy is beautiful. The road to Lismore is special, particularly in Spring and Autumn. Lismore Castle is imposing and moody and the scenic route to Dungarvan also a treat and from here, a ferry runs daily to Wexford. There are two roads that run parallel, the top road being the more beautiful. When I was young and fit I used to run from Fermoy to The Blue Dragon

Inn, a steep climb. It was here that I trained for my first Dublin City Marathon and would subsequently run in two more. I ran all around Kilworth where I had a friend in the training camp. I often expressed a wish to own a house up from the river. My friend married a local schoolteacher and they moved into a house up from the river – living my dream.

I eventually left Fermoy in 1982 because of the differences of opinion with my boss and I headed for the Curragh with a heavy heart. I knew that it had been my inflexibility that had caused the rift and I was sick with regret. The latest news from Lebanon seemed to match my gloom. Israel had attacked Lebanon on June 6, 1982, stating that that it wanted to put a stop on the raids aimed at Israeli territory from Southern Lebanon. By the end of the first week of fighting, the International Red Cross and Lebanese police figures claimed that almost ten thousand people had died and almost seventeen thousand had been injured. By the end of the second week, the numbers had increased to fourteen thousand deaths and twenty thousand injured, mostly civilians. As the war dragged on UN peacekeepers were caught in the middle.

But the war in Lebanon seemed very far away as the first snow of winter blanketed the open ground and the hollows across the Curragh. Every evening I drove home to Dublin, listening to the car radio. One evening as I drove across the snow-covered Curragh Plains under a moonlit sky, I heard Luciano Pavarotti singing the Christmas carol, 'O Holy Night', composed by Adolphe Adam. I was overcome with emotion. Something in that magnificent tenor voice touched me deeply. Pavarotti's technique was exceptional. There is also a recording on DVD of the Italian maestro performing in the Royal Albert Hall in the presence of the Queen Mother and Queen Elizabeth II and it is extraordinary. A Jose Carreras performance from La Scala, Milan, 1985 is also a textbook study of a tenor who, though small in stature, uses every centimetre of his being (including standing on this tiptoe) to produce the most marvellous sound in Giordano's *Andrea Chenier*, *Un di all'azzurro spazio*, a poem in praise of love, beauty and the earth. A masterclass in the art of the tenor. Before I left the Curragh Plains and joined the Naas Dual Carriageway my love affair with classical music had been reignited.

Nine months after the incident in the wadi in Lebanon I was called to a court martial in Limerick. Our second-in-command was representing the two reprobates who had threatened me in Deir Ntar by 'offering violence to an officer', to put it in military terms. I was questioned by the Board and I perceived their questioning as hostile and it irritated me. The two were found guilty of partaking of unprescribed drugs. One received fourteen days' detention. I cannot remember what was meted out to the other one. They were lucky. In 1981 two privates were on duty close to the platoon house that we had occupied in Deir Ntar. Private Hugh Doherty was shot in the back and killed. His companion, Private Kevin Joyce was kidnapped. He has never been found.

There were two reports on that Deir Ntar incident, one by the United Nations, not disclosed to the public and one by Major General Vincent Savino, in 1984, also restricted. Following continued representations by the Doherty and Joyce families and the publication of a book in 2013 by Frank Sumner, a former member of the defence forces and one of the last people to see Privates Doherty and Joyce alive, the then Minister for Defence, Simon Coveney commissioned Mr Justice Roderick Murphy to carry out an investigation into the circumstances of the deaths. The Murphy Report was finally published in June 2018, thirty-seven years after the killings in Deir Ntar. It is a damning account of errors on the part of the defence forces' command and a public apology was made by the Minister to the bereaved families. From my reading of the report, not only do I conclude that serious 'errors' were made by the officers on the ground but that a combination of gross incompetence and lack of empathy for enlisted soldiers was to blame. Two young soldiers on a listening post, on an exposed mound, an unprotected OP is nothing short of criminal and the Battalion Commander must take sole responsibility for their deaths. No lessons were learned from the killing, the previous year of Privates Smallhorne and Barrett and two young, inexperienced soldiers were posted on a reverse slope of a wadi in Deir Ntar, with no visible contact with the Platoon Post and with no NCO. Mahmoud Bazzi, a member of the DFF was deported from the USA in 2015 to stand trial for the murder of Privates Smallhorne and Barrett. The outcome has yet to be determined.

Over the next fourteen years, peacekeepers would encounter some of the worst incidents of the wars that continued between Israeli and rebel fighters. Fighting was relentless, and thousands of civilians fled their homes to seek refuge in the UN compounds situated between the two opposing and deadly forces. Without food or water, the majority had taken to the roads – in clapped-out vehicles or on foot – and were mowed down by crossfire. UN troops helped evacuate people, including the dead and injured from dozens of villages where families were trapped by the constant bombardment and delivered food and water wherever they could, unsure themselves if they would make it back to safety. They assisted the ambulance service in removing dismembered corpses from the roadside, from wadis and from the crushed remains of family homes in and around the villages, often having to abandon search and rescue or clean-up operations as more artillery rained down from the Israeli hilltop bases and counter fire rose from Hezbullah-occupied wadis and dug-outs on the other side. What they had to deal with was horrendous – images, sounds and tasks that would affect the rest of their lives.

During 'Operation Grapes of Wrath', in April 1996 Israeli Defence Force artillery shells struck a Fijian UN compound where eight hundred civilians had taken refuge from the fighting. At least a hundred and twenty people died. Soldier, award-winning poet and historian, Cpl. Michael J. Whelan, who served in Lebanon, recorded in poetry some harrowing images from Irish soldiers' time there. One of the most poignant and heart-wrenching poems from his collection, *Peacekeeper* is called 'Grapes of Wrath'

A soldier climbs from the rubbled limbs
and discarded faces, his eyes caked with tears,
his hands at arm's length clutching the newborn baby
that looks like a headless doll.

Grapes of Wrath, Michael J. Whelan – *Peacekeeper,* 2016

CHAPTER 6

Saved by the Air Corps

I am forever chained to the Via Dolorosa

Jerusalem, Michael J. Whelan

Having returned to the Curragh, and the smell of the turf fires, I began the 15th Young Officers' Course in September 1983. I enjoyed the Military College. The Administrative element always seemed to be in trouble and I thought it my duty to help them get out of it. Getting my teeth into projects would occupy my mind. Looking for shortcomings of any sort would enable me to fix something; I was beyond fixing. The experience I had gained at the bicycle shop in Dublin, where I had worked in my youth now came to the fore. The Military College had a large store room that had about fifty unused bicycles, all in various stages of disrepair. I managed to extract thirty of them and have them restored and I loaned them to the 1st Cavalry Squadron for a weekend cycling trip out into the hills. I was editor of the class magazine (I suppose it might be called a 'year book' as there was just one edition for the year) which I also enjoyed. I had a men's club constructed, including a bar. It went well. Years later, on my posting out in 1984, I was complimented by the College Commandant, Colonel Tom Waters on its operation. In a letter to me dated the 27th of July 1984 he said, "I fully appreciate the difficulties you may have encountered in getting the construction work completed and in the provision of barrack service equipment. You have done this in a most efficient manner without recourse to higher authority. You can be assured that the men whose morale has been boosted will fully appreciate your work on their behalf". His words were very gratifying and helped boost my own morale in no small measure.

I asked Mick O'Brien to take a photograph of the 'Falling Plates' competition, a competition for which a high level of fitness is required, an event in which several teams compete, running three hundred yards to a point that is hundred yards from a target – the butt of the range, where up to eight metal plates for each team are placed. Each man had a pre-selected plate which he had to knock and then turn his attention to any remaining plates that were still standing. There is a 'pivot man' – the best shot – who is chosen to knock everything standing. The trophy is a statuette of a soldier, called Paddy Scully, after an FCA man – a 'sandbag' – a rather derisive term used by full-timers to refer to part-time soldiers. Mick O'Brien's photo became the reference photo for a watercolour painting called 'The Falling Plates', painted by the artist, Pat Phelan. I presented the painting to the Officers' Mess at Fitzgerald Camp in Fermoy, in County Cork in 1987. I enjoyed the course and although the food was rather poor, a few drinks in our own mess in the evening compensated. There were a few people who brought a little light, one of them being the Dean, John Patterson, a lovely man, spiritually genuine, who had toured India.

But my time at the college was not without its problems. I had run-ins with some, some of the Cadet School officers about night observation devices (NODs) that hadn't been returned to the 3rd Battalion. The Third had complained to the Operations Commandant. I hadn't signed for them and told him that I had no responsibility for them. He was not pleased.

It was my first experience of someone's displeasure and it rattled me. I was asked to pose for a class photograph but the Administration Officer, who had been a classmate, wasn't happy with the photograph because I was wearing a shirt and tie; he wanted one of me in Service Dress Number 1 – Sam Browne belt and jacket. I told him to f---off. I was a QM and should have been treated with more respect. There had been a lot of water under a lot of bridges since my training days as a seventeen-year-old recruit; the 'timid little bastard' had grown up – or so he thought.

All of this must have been overlooked by the course commander whose comments on my performance included, 'a composed personality who related very well to his fellow students, a positive attitude to the course throughout, though of a quiet disposition, when called on to contribute to class discussion, he invariably had a pertinent comment to make. A dependable officer'. Like my earlier class report, this one lay neatly in a file, unseen by me until many years later.

I had been headhunted for the Quartermaster's Branch, Infirmary Road, Dublin, in 1984 mainly because I had done a longevity study of cadet uniform sizes including caps 29A, used by cadets when on guards of honour dignitaries of Church and State. There was a shortage and units sent fictional numbers to Army Headquarters. Based on my report the QMG's staff decided that I should be working with them in Planning. I knew one of the officers because we had attended UCD together. When I arrived, he briefed me on the job, then promptly resigned! I did ex-post analysis of the budget using Pie charts. The balance between pay and non-pay was always an issue. But soon, I was bored in the Quartermaster General's Branch. Besides, there were two civil servants with whom I met once a month to agree recruitment of civilian employees as per the Quartermaster General's priorities. I hated these two. While posted as duty officer in Defence Forces Headquarters I had access to a store room stuffed with weapons and ammunition and I would fantasise about meeting them, armed with a pistol, and putting two neat holes in each of them! They were spared because I was busy selecting academic courses for staff, relevant to the logistician's job and I was involved in the sub-committee on computerisation of stores which took me away on a few 'swan trips': trips down the country – with 'mileage'. But this would be the twilight of my career. I had no contact with troops. I was a civil servant in uniform and I was missing the Military College.

Depression was a term that I had lately come to understand as the name for my state of mind. I had 'negative thoughts' and the incidences of urges to end my life were increasing. I was working next door to the army psychologist who specialised in courses. I liked him as a person, but I didn't speak to him about my issues. I didn't speak to anyone. I could never be at ease. I needed something else to fill the hours so that I wouldn't have to remember Jerusalem More than anything, I wanted to make some sense of what had happened to me. I went back to college to study psychology and mathematics – again at UCD. I had always had an aptitude for mathematics but this time I failed. I was unable to concentrate, and I reverted to a single subject and a single course – a BA in Psychology. The study took me some way towards understanding human behaviour and while it helped me to see and deal with some of my own issues, it left many questions unanswered. For instance, I don't know if I will ever understand the mind that can inflict such violence as sexual assault on another human being. The best I could achieve was an uneasy acceptance of what had happened to me.

Albert Camus's book, *The Myth of Sisyphus* was a life saver. Camus suggested that 'once stripped of its common romanticism, the world is a foreign, strange and inhuman place. 'True knowledge is impossible, and rationality and science cannot reveal the world. Such explanations ultimately end in meaningless abstractions and metaphors. The absurd arises when the human need to understand meets the unreasonableness of the world'. Further, Camus answered what he considered to be the only question of philosophy that mattered: does the realisation of the meaninglessness and absurdity of life necessarily require suicide? His answer is 'No'. Instead, he says that it requires revolt, and that reason and its limits must be acknowledged without false hope. Like Sisyphus, a figure in Greek mythology who was condemned to repeat forever the same meaningless task of pushing a boulder up a mountain only to see it roll down again, I abandoned hope of ever making sense of, or overcoming my suffering, and tried to accept that I was a broken person, that I would remain broken – destroyed forever – and to get on with life as it was, to the best of my ability and embrace all that the unreasonable world had to offer.

In 1985, at forty years of age, I was promoted to Captain. Some of my Potential Officers' class would be promoted to Commandant when they turned fifty. In 1985, the Quartermaster General considered me suitable for promotion to Commandant, but ten years seemed a long time; 1995 seemed a long way off. I was not too good, mentally at this stage and I didn't want to wait. A decision to leave the army was forming in my mind. The 'Situations Vacant' pages of Friday's *Irish Times* became a must read. One Friday I spotted an advertisement for a Higher Executive Officer and an Executive Officer with the Medical Council. The previous incumbent was an assistant principal civil servant who had left to take up a position with the newly established Irish College of General Practitioners. In mid-May 1986 I was HEO in the Medical Council, a statutory body whose roots went back to the General Medical Council, 44, Hallam Street, London. All former colonies of the British Empire have medical councils: The Pakistan Medical and Dental Council, Medical Council of India, South Africa, New Zealand and Australia. Each Council is responsible for discipline, education and training, supervision of hospital training and all medical bodies are under their rule. There is a strict code of ethics. There are committees – of registration, education and training, fitness to practice and finance – and each committee has a chairmen and members, usually determined by statute. The public interest is paramount.

I was responsible for preparing briefs for quarterly Council meetings. Council meetings were held at Broc House on Nutley Lane. The food was excellent, and I considered it a privilege to be amongst these knowledgeable professors of medicine – even the grumpy ones. In the beginning, I got along well but interpersonal staff issues eventually caused problems. Two of the girls were members of IMPACT trade union. We were members of IBEC, the employers' organisation who would negotiate on our behalf. My boss hated unions. I believed in compromise, my boss seemed to thrive on conflict. I was piggy in the middle. When we changed to computerised accounts and paid off the woman who had done the accounts manually for years, she was distraught. There was nothing the union or I could do for her. Fortunately, she had served long enough to receive a pension. We established a fund for future pensions. All of us worked our arses off until we were burned out. Whenever the boss went on holiday, I'd order a cake and we'd meet in the club room for coffee and craic. I had no previous experience working with girls, but I found that I got along really well with them. According to them I wasn't 'bossy'. The typing pool was eventually moved to the top of the building, facing the Jesuit's Hostel. One day I caught the girls huddled in a bunch, looking out the window from where they had an eyeful of the boys showering in the hostel. The boss would not have been pleased. I cautioned them not to keep this up and they took it in good spirits.

Expense records could be diverse – and contentious. One committee member took a train from Cork and only claimed the cost of his train fare, while another drove from Bantry in a Mercedes and claimed mileage. But nice lunch meetings, hosted by the president, with wine before meetings enables sticky issues to be overcome in a diplomatic fashion. Some of the medical professionals could be quite brash and undiplomatic, which left me somewhat shocked. When I asked one gynaecologist to join an inspection team he said to me, "What's the matter Chris? Jump up on the couch and take down your knickers." I said nothing. Some people hated him. "Pin-striped suit and a flower" some called him. Others referred to him as "that pup".

As well as attending meetings and servicing Council meetings I looked after the registration committee, the education and training committee, the computer section and general administration. I had a row with my boss over the Annual Report in which I omitted the name of a pathologist. I made the error because he was giving me a hard time and because of this I was under pressure. Soon after that incident he reprimanded me because my signature on documents was 'too large'. This was the straw that broke the camel's back. A sudden, immense episode of depersonalisation hit me, the worst episode that I had since Deir Ntar. As I was still an Army Reserve officer, I could use the showers at Army HQ, I ran, choking for breath, trying not to fall flat on my face and I stood under a shower to give myself some time to come to. The episode took a long time to pass.

The final blow came some weeks later as we were interviewing candidates for the position of executive officer. During the interview with a female candidate I made some notes and asked the usual boring questions. A few months later, the Equality Authority wrote to the Council saying that the lady had been asked a sexist question while being interviewed by two male board members. An Emergency Meeting was called, attended by all the board members as well as a solicitor, and Senior and Junior Counsel. Suddenly all eyes fell on me. Our solicitor said, "You will have to take the stand and be sworn." "No problem," I replied, "I didn't ask the lady the sexist question but if the lady said that she was asked a sexist question we must believe her. I wouldn't be so stupid as to ask a sexist question". But my goose was cooked. The boss circumvented me at every turn. By now I was very sick, and I knew that I must leave the Council. I handed in my letter of resignation and I was given three months' salary in advance and my contributions to the pension fund were returned. My career was over. The clarity of hindsight is marvellous; I couldn't take correction, nor could I be challenged. I had moved from the 'frying pan' that was the army and into the fire and like a wounded animal, I was angry – and I was now unemployable.

To pass the time I began running again. I had been long-distance running for years and I had run three marathons. Now, the running filled a few hours each day and of course the exercise helped me feel better. At the same time, I sent CVs here, there and everywhere. I did three interviews with the Opticians Board, Overseas Aid, and Forfás, the National Policy Advisory Board for Enterprise, Trade, Science, Technology and Innovation. At each interview my reason for leaving my last job always cropped up. "Why did you leave the Medical Council?" the interviewer asked. "Because my boss was an asshole" was what I wanted to say but of course I didn't say that. I told the interviewer in Forfás that I had a fertile mind. "What exactly do you mean by this?" he asked. "One can plant new ideas in it," I replied. To me, my answer made perfect sense but to the interviewer, it seemed to make absolutely no sense whatsoever. I should have simply told him that I had an enquiring mind and that after four years in the Council I felt I needed a change – something new and challenging. But I tended to talk in shorthand, expecting the person I talked with to fill in the gaps. I hated being questioned for any reason. Unsurprisingly, none of my interviews resulted in employment and I plummeted further into the depths of depression.

I had been more than a year without work when a former colleague who now worked in the Irish Air Corps at Baldonnel advised me that jobs with the Air Corps for civilian employees had been advertised through FÁS, the then semi-state training and employment agency. I rang FÁS and was told that the competition was closed. But, after some persuasion I succeeded in having my name added to the list. I did a preliminary interview in the FÁS office in Clondalkin, followed by an interview conducted by an Air Corps officer and a civil servant in Irish Air Corps HQ in Baldonnel Aerodrome. The board of FÁS had reservations. Given that I was a former manager I was deemed to be over qualified. Could I step down to employee level? Would I get on with my new peers? Would I be happy with much less pay? I must have assured them that I could and would because I was offered the job and was happy to take it. I was more than grateful to have any job that would occupy my mind and provide an income at last.

By now, I had watched all, but one of my six siblings marry and leave home. As their families arrived I became the bachelor uncle – and godfather to one nephew. Together with my sister, I looked after our parents who had become more precious as they aged. My mother's health began to suffer, and she was diagnosed with Chronic Obstructive Pulmonary Disease (COPD), a progressive lung disease that made it difficult for her to breathe. This came as quite a shock to all of us, especially as my mother had never been a smoker. Some of the hospital staff at St James's Hospital put it down to breathing in coal fumes and dust from our fireplace at home and we came to the same conclusion, realising – too late, of course – that the old chimney had always given trouble. I watched her struggle during the weeks before her death. I had known fear and I believed that I had overcome this impostor, but dread was more sinister. While driving through Stillorgan in South Dublin I saw a coffin being driven in a hearse. The lid of the coffin was open. I was overcome with a feeling of impending doom. Before my mother died in 1997 I was walking towards her ward when I overheard two nurses talking. One of them told the other that "Mrs McQuaid had blood poisoning". I jumped to the conclusion that it was due to complications from MRSA, the infamous hospital bug, probably contracted in the hospital and this made me angry. I did night shifts by her bed. I spoke to her even though she couldn't hear me. I prayed non-stop for fourteen days, alas to no avail. When my mother died my faith died too. I believe that losing a parent is a greater blow to us in adulthood because we are at the point where we are actually friends with them.

On the day that my mother died I sat in my room and played the *Largo* from Beethoven's 9th Symphony (choral) on CD. I had always turned to classical music in times of darkness. My mother and I shared a love of classical music and I suppose I was trying to reach out to connect with her in some forlorn way, trying to make sense of her passing, trying to keep something of her in the empty place inside, trying to purge the feeling of doom. I wanted to avoid having to accept that she was gone and that nothing and no-one could ever take her place.

In the midst of grieving, I had administrative issues with the local church. While her remains could repose in the Dominican church known as The Priory in the old Tallaght village, it would be one of the priests from the smaller parish where we now lived who would officiate at her funeral Mass. To say that this nonsense annoyed me would be an understatement. I saw this as a snub and I had nothing but contempt for these people. However, years later they were redeemed by a Dominican priest, Fr Richard whom I accompanied to the Wagner Festival in Bayreuth, Germany for a performance of my beloved *Parsifal*. He loved it. I have a card that he sent me afterwards and I treasure it. I had spent a short time with him the day before he died – St Stephen's day – a number of years ago. To me he was a saint.

My father lived for another thirteen years after my mother died. I was his personal chef. He loved rib-roast beef, cabbage and roast potatoes. I cooked a goose for his eightieth birthday which he relished. But I could never interest him in Opera. On the one occasion that he watched it on TV I had pampered him all day – full Irish breakfast, broth for lunch and a rib roast for dinner. I wanted him to hear one piece in particular: the *Duetto-Sul Aria* from *The Marriage of Figaro* used in recent years in the film, *The Shawshank Redemption*. I called him minutes before the scene was due to open. He hobbled into the living room and sat down, watched the scene, lasting about ten minutes, then stood up. "What's for tea?" he asked as he hobbled off again. On the morning of his death I awoke early and had a shower and then noticed that I was having a nosebleed. This was something new. On the way to the hospital to see my father I received a call from a nurse who told me that my father had 'taken a turn'. When I arrived, he was dead. I finally got to see him but not without an argument with a staff nurse. I was red-faced and in trouble. I was now panicking because the special hydraulic bed supplied by the Health Board that my father had been using during his illness was still in our living room. I asked for the bed to be removed from our house because his remains would be coming home. The bed was taking up the room where his coffin would be placed. The Health Board people were in no hurry. I rang them one more time and said that unless the bed was removed by two o'clock that afternoon I would use an angle grinder to dismantle it myself. Soon afterwards, the bed was collected but by then I had worked myself into a frenzy. That night, a heart rate of c.140bpm forced me back to hospital. I also had a chest infection. The consultant on call wanted to admit me. "My father is at home in a box," I told him. Tanked to the eyeballs on strong antibiotics, I could barely stand at my father's funeral Mass the next day, but I wanted to say some words to honour his memory. I remembered the 'opera incident' which brought a smile to the faces of the congregation, particularly those who knew him well.

I have no fear of dying but the death of a beloved family member or a close friend is a different kettle of fish. It is very painful. The wound of the loss can return with a memory, a comment or a piece of music. I believed that what makes life bearable is the certain knowledge that we too will die. According to Marietta in *Die tote Stadt* by Erich Wolfgang Korngold, "life is to be lived" but with both my parents gone, I was left with a hollow feeling inside and I knew that without them life from now on would be difficult. I was grateful to have my job with the Air Corps and my friends at Baldonnel. But the ten years that I had spent in the main technical stores had been difficult. I tended to make life hard for myself and even here, I was over zealous and anxious – and quick to pull people up on anything that appeared to be 'off kilter'. I had a row over LR6 batteries – of all things. A pack of four was the norm but one company supplied five in a pack. I accidentally came onto this when the man who looked after batteries was on sick leave. I researched it and took the batteries, four hundred and eighty in all, on charge by certified receipt voucher. There was holy blue murder. The supervisor sent for me and asked for an explanation. I told him that any surplus must be taken on charge. He wasn't happy. I was accused of bullying one of my colleagues. He was supported by the Union shop steward. An envelope with my name on it was slipped through a sliding window in my work area while I was at lunch. It had come from Personnel requesting me to attend a meeting to answer the charge of bullying. They had the complaint on the account of one witness. I was furious. My union, SIPTU took up the case and I was given a month's leave with pay and a transfer to Heli Wing. One of my friends, 'The Professor" said "Oh, didn't Mister McQuaid get a severe punishment – a month off with pay and a transfer." It had been a close call and I tried my best to stay out of trouble from then on. Fortunately, the last ten years as a logistician with the Heli Wing were a delight. The technicians were the best – good in their hearts and very skilled. The pilots too were very friendly, and it was a privilege to work with them. Although Heli Wing was bliss, I had a lot of work to do and with the help of the wonderful technicians, it was completed by the time I left Baldonnel in 2010. As a former member of the Defence Forces I received no preferential treatment at Baldonnel but I have the highest respect for the technical people in the Irish Air Corps. They are professionals who rate second only to my beloved 1st Motor Squadron in Fermoy. But by 2010, I was burned out – not from work but from a long and wearisome struggle that robbed me of energy and any ability to cope with retirement.

Chris McQuaid at Curragh Military Barracks
prior to departure for Cyprus, 1964

Chris McQuaid (left) and Pte. Pat Walsh
at Mt. Juliet, Cyprus, January 1965

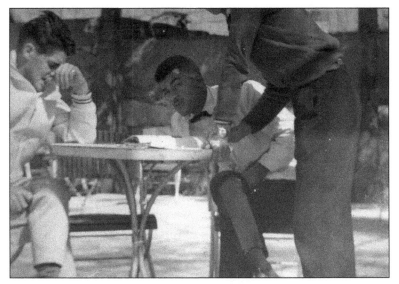

Chris McQuaid (left) at hotel in Jerusalem,
morning of 15th February 1965

Chris McQuaid in the Holy Land 17th February 1965

Chris McQuaid (left) and
Pte. Francis Browne, kneeling
at the Church of the Nativity
17th February 1965

Chris McQuaid,
Cyprus March 1965

Chris McQuaid in Lefka, Cyprus, April 1965

CHAPTER 7

The Last Battle

*Many times I have witnessed the caravans
leave the City of Heaven
and I longed to go home, un-scourged.*

Jerusalem, Michael J. Whelan

Six months after the assault in Jerusalem, the perpetrator was married. Nine years later, the NCO told me that he had informed two officers of the incident and had made a statement to the sexual abuse unit of An Gárda Síochána at Harcourt Street. He said that they had interviewed the accused and he had denied it. By this time, I had also made a statement to the Gárdaí but the Director of Public Prosecutions said that the case couldn't be brought to court because the incident had occurred in a foreign jurisdiction. No investigation was carried out within the army. I am guessing that if it had been reported to authorities in Jerusalem, both the rapist and I would have been beheaded.

People who have been raped or sexually abused live inside cracked shells, covered with plaster and painted over so that the cracks cannot be seen. To outsiders, the pain may be invisible and sometimes it is invisible, even to the conscious mind of the victim. But the unconscious mind knows about it and out of the blue, the unconscious becomes conscious and the victim is re-traumatised. Anger, borne of a fractured persona and memories deeply buried, led me into to an alcohol phase that was like climbing a greasy pole. I also had an eating disorder, from which I had recovered through re-education from 1969 to 1977. But as time passed I was plagued by obsessional behaviour, manifesting in failure to let go of an argument, writing irate, complaining letters, having arguments with employers and learning to hate. Hate became an indulgence and yet I craved acceptance and union with someone – someone who would personify the undefiled, whole and stable human being that I had lost. I joined a dating agency but failure to function as a man brought only rejection. Like the fabled Humpty Dumpty I was beyond repair.

No-one seemed to notice; at least, no-one said anything – until October 1992, not long after I began working at Baldonnel, when a friend of mine, a fellow army officer said that I had 'changed drastically'! I clammed up and didn't press him to elaborate any further, perhaps afraid that he, or someone else would have me committed to a mental institution. My biggest fear was that I would lose my job. Although I was still in my forties and still fairly physically fit, I gathered from my friend's observation of my demeanour that I was unfit for work. Astute that he was, my friend advised me to apply for a disability pension. "I have no knowledge of the application procedure," I said, lamely. He scribbled a number on a piece of paper and handed it to me. "Ring Eileen," he said.

Eileen sent me an application form. The application for a disability pension seemed like a straightforward procedure. I outlined the circumstances of the assault in Jerusalem, resulting in post-traumatic stress disorder, respiratory issues that had lasted since I had pneumonia and pleurisy in Cyprus as well as a hearing problem that had manifested at an early stage when, as a young soldier, training on the Vickers machine gun, I was lying in the lowest position underneath the weapon, rolling my head from side to side, trying to ease the pain in my head from the deafening explosions. I was not alone as regards hearing problems; hundreds of army men paid a high price, their hearing damaged for life. Captain Cathal O'Neill was the first officer that I had seen wearing ear protection during an all-army competition at the Curragh and I witnessed an officer from

Operations ordering Cathal to remove it!

With the application form completed, I signed it and sent it off, expecting to be called for a medical examination and an interview or a discussion before being granted my pension. Having been examined by the Pensions Board doctor in 1993, I was sent to an Army Medical Corps psychiatrist, then in a training post at St Patrick's Hospital, who found some evidence of Post-Traumatic Stress but reported that I 'failed to fulfil the criteria for the complete PTSD' and I was referred to a senior psychologist who carried out a test, effectively a box-ticking exercise. His report stated that I was 'immature'. A GP I had seen in Fermoy then arranged for me to see an eminent psychiatrist in Cork who only saw private patients after hours. The psychiatrist in Cork found that I was suffering from PTSD 'in a profound way'. My friend, Eoin Kelly and his wife Mary collected me after my appointment and put me up in their home, a kindness that I shall never forget.

I submitted this report to the Army Pensions Board. I was deemed eighty percent disabled – attributable to service. But nothing happened. It would be many years later before I discovered, under the Freedom of Information Act that the Pensions Policy Section of the Board, the section responsible for the formulation and review of pension policy, legislation and schemes had criticised the board for the award and questioned the sexual assault. They said that because I was 'on holiday' in Jerusalem in 1965 it didn't count. The life-threatening incident in the wadi in Lebanon was of little interest to them.

Between November 1994 and March 1995, a number of representations were made by public representatives on my behalf to find out what was the cause of the delay – to no avail. As I awaited the Board's determination, my disability had been downgraded to fifty percent then to zero percent, then altered to a fifteen percent, then back to thirty percent. I knew none of this this. Finally, I received a letter signed by the Administrator of the Pensions Board informing me that my case had not succeeded. It was then that I went, under the Freedom of Information Act, to the APB and to the army for my service record. A second Board was convened, headed by a medical examiner. I received a letter from Pensions Administration rejecting my claim and stating that I was thirty percent disabled but this was likely 'due to a pre-existing condition prior to enlistment'. I eventually instructed my legal advisor and in due course, Mr Justice Barr granted my application for a judicial review. Following this, I received a phone call from the Pensions Board Administrator telling me bluntly that if I lost the case the State would pursue me for costs and I would in all likelihood, be sent to prison! At this time, I was being pursued for legal costs by my solicitor. I sought a bank loan but was refused. I also wrote to the Association of Retired Commissioned Officers for help. Three months later I received a refusal, but they wished me well.

Once the case was listed for a full hearing in the High Court the State entered into secret talks with my Senior Counsel and I was requested to present myself to yet another army psychiatrist at St. Bricin's Hospital. I was reluctant to do this but following legal advice, I eventually agreed. The outcome was an acknowledgement of fifty percent disability attributable to service and an award of a disability pension in accordance with the findings. At the time, I couldn't come to any conclusion other than that this was a sinister move to reduce the impact of my complaint and the cost to the State. Words used in the APB report are inaccurate. For instance, it stated that the corporal who had assisted me in the wadi in Lebanon was a 'senior NCO'. This is factually untrue. He was a junior NCO. This lack of military knowledge and lack of attention to detail by Administration was one thing; lack of understanding and empathy was even greater.

Contrary to the opinion of the psychiatrist at St. Bricin's Hospital whose report stated that things couldn't have been so bad given my achievements at school and university and my rapid rise through the ranks, the sexual assault had a devastating effect on my life including my ability to think, to interact with people in a normal fashion and to have normal sexual relations. There was no understanding that in an effort to survive, I had to keep my mind occupied. I welcomed the opportunity to return to education, even while suffering severe and debilitating bouts of depression – and at the same time, working as an officer. It had been extremely difficult for me, but I had succeeded in getting through to my degree. As regards rising in the ranks, I had not sought a commission; I had been *selected* for commissioning.

I had a feeling that this report was essentially written by Pensions Administration to minimise the severity of my condition and cheat me out of the eighty percent award that was originally granted to me in 1993. This case took almost nine years from 1992 to 2001 and in my opinion, was tantamount to a cover-up by agents of the Irish State. My claim was never solely about monetary gain. If I was unfit for work, I simply wanted enough to live on and some sort of acknowledgement by the defence forces that I had suffered physical, psychological and emotional injury while serving as a soldier overseas. It had taken me years to come to terms with the shock of the assault in Jerusalem, but I had managed to make some progress – albeit faltering and fragile – through university. Because of having earned a degree, I had risen through the ranks in the army to become a commissioned officer. The incident in Lebanon put paid to any hope of continuing my career. Neither the crime in Jerusalem nor the threat in Lebanon was committed by an outside force but from *within the Irish Defence Forces*. The fact that the sexual predator could not be brought to justice had eaten away every shred of human dignity, leading to a lifetime of physical, mental and emotional torture. I wanted the Irish Defence Forces to be accountable. I met him once since that awful incident in Jerusalem. It was at Collins Barracks. I was carrying a rifle, mercifully unloaded. As he passed me, he grinned.

The cumulative effects of the stress induced by the lengthy legal wrangle, the financial burden of legal and other costs and the injustice suffered at the hands of those in power had served to bring me close to total destruction. My health issues worsened, necessitating frequent visits to doctors. Eventually, having obtained some compensation and costs, I began attending psychiatric services, as a private patient. This was getting me nowhere and again, I sought out some way to occupy my mind. The sense of team spirit, fraternity, and common purpose had sustained me in the army and still appealed to me enormously and I joined the Cavalry Club, an officers' club, founded in 1944 and authorised by the military authorities in 1946. Membership is open to all serving and retired commissioned cavalry officers of the Permanent Defence Force and the Army Reserve and members pay an annual subscription of twenty-five Euro. Members of the committee are elected at the Club's Annual General Meeting. The current tenure of office is for one year and the club's president presents a report at the Annual General Meeting, which takes place during the month of December. Under the chair of the club's president the committee arranges functions and activities it deems appropriate to the achievement of the club's objectives. A programme of events is published on a yearly basis. Activities include visiting battlefields, annual Saint Brigid's Day celebrations and attending parades and national and regional commemorations. In recent years the club has conducted an overseas tour of battlefields in Belgium and France. Other activities include lectures, visits to museums and an annual golf competition for club members, including their spouses or partners. Club members also frequently avail of activities organised by the McKee Officers Club such as theatre outings and tours.

As well as the need for social activity and comradeship, I was also drawn to the ethos of the club which was originally established to provide a refuge for officers who were being demobbed after the

'Emergency' (1939-1945). St Brigid was selected as Patron because the club was formed in the Curragh in County Kildare where St. Brigid founded her first monastery. A St. Brigid's Cross features on the president's chain of office. Brigid is renowned for her hospitality and hard work and her cheerful, generous giving of food and shelter. As a woman of God and a woman of the people, a powerful personality who appealed to all – from those in high places to the humble beggar – she was the most appropriate symbol that would set the standard for the hospitality of a place where individuals were made welcome. I believe that RDF (Reserve Defence Force Officers) should be granted associate membership status only and that professional cavalry officers who go overseas and take risks to life and limb should be the only ordinary members.

I became president in 2001. I began by designing headed notepaper as well as a Certificate of Honorary Membership which I had framed. I also created a framed Certificate of Honorary Membership for General Nash who would later wear the hat that had been worn by the late Dermot Earley, Chief of Staff of the Defence Forces. I used to joke with Dermot Early about the 'Nasher' wearing his hat. General Nash had received a *Legion D'Orde* while he was in charge of African operations and stationed in Paris and the cap sported the two rows of oak leaves with a gold badge, identical to the cap worn by our Chief of Staff. The 11th Cavalry (now dissolved) had a big input into the club and I used to call it "The Eleventh Cavalry Club".

While I was president, I invited Seán Hennessey, former Squadron Commander, 1st Motor Squadron to the Reconnection dinner. Seán served in the Congo as captain with the Armoured Element in the 35th Battalion in 1961. Art Magennis, DSM was in Seán's section. They lost two members of the battalion during fighting in Elizabethville in 1961. Michael Nolan who was killed in action and eighteen-year-old Trooper Patrick Mullins is still recorded as 'Missing in Action'.

Seán recently celebrated the 70th anniversary of his commissioning in Cork. I loved these two old soldiers. I am still in contact with Seán Hennessey and with Art Magennis. They were like grandfathers to me – and beloved of the Cavalry Corps. Former O/C, Commandant Thomas Kelly, 1st Motor Squadron was also invited to the Reconnection Dinner. Kelly is said to have hidden bombs under the altar in the church in Fermoy, causing panic when it was learned that the bishop was about to visit the church on a tour of inspection. He was a wit with a great sense of humour, famous for a quip to a local farmer who had complained that a horse was grazing in a field leased from the army for grazing his sheep. Kelly accompanied the farmer to the field in question. Sure enough, a horse was grazing happily amongst the sheep. "Now tell me," the farmer began, "Is that a horse over there?" Kelly looked at him with a twinkle in his eye. "How the hell do I know? I'm an army officer, not a vet!"

But as time went on, the club rules were amended which reinforced its exclusiveness as an officer's only club, a club that is not registered, is not under control of military management and yet has the use of State property for free – a private members club. My troubles began when I asked for a cash account and everyone went ballistic, resulting in prolonged correspondence of a bitter nature until it was decided to expel me from the club by way of Rule 6, a convoluted and non-democratic rule which stated: 'In case the conduct of any member, either within or out of the Club shall, in the opinion of the Committee or any twenty members of the Club, who shall certify same in writing, be injurious to the character and interests of the Club, after such request, having firstly given the member written details of the complaint made against him/her and an invitation to appear before the Committee to answer any complaints made against him/her. After such a request and invitation, and where the member does not resign, the Committee shall then call a Special General Meeting and if a majority of two-thirds of those present and voting, vote for the expulsion of such member, he/she shall cease to be a Member of the Club'. A Committee meeting was convened – twelve against one and no third party allowed. The venue for the meeting was the UN School in the Curragh, ironically, the School for International Peace.

I now viewed the Cavalry Club as a nest of snobbery with no legal status per se – although it is recognised by the Minister for Defence and the army authorities. I was not from similar background to the rest of the members and I was the first president of the club to be appointed from the ranks. I considered myself well educated, cultured and civilised and someone who would take no shit from anyone, irrespective of rank. But the latter approach was not well received. I was ostracised and eventually I was left with no choice but to resign – or be expelled.

It was around this time that I suffered my first heart attack. But I continued working, I continued running the Wagner Society of Ireland – which I had also founded – and I was helping my sister to look after my father. The work at Baldonnel filled the week and the Wagner Society gave me focus. Wagner had become a passion – and I believed it would be my saviour – but within a very short time, unease started to creep in. Some of the members were beginning to get up my nose and things were not going my way. I was feeling disrespected, unappreciated and let down. Some members of the society began to die off, among them four of my supporters whose presence had been a comfort to me. They liked me. I simply wasn't liked by the rest of them and I reacted to their dislike by admonishing them, through what they took as rudeness. I didn't care. My perception was one of 'me against the world'. Now my physical health was letting me down and it had become a cause for concern. Ousted from the Cavalry Club and Wagner Society, I had to deal with serious health problems: prostate cancer, Type 2 diabetes and recurring heart arrhythmia, and I took risks travelling to mainland Europe to attend Wagner operas because I needed something to do. I tried to just get on with everything. I had grown into the mask that I thought I was presenting to the world. but I could not ignore the gnawing yearning for the person I once was when I was nineteen – happy and carefree – before *the Hosannas ended.* I wanted my life back.

In 2016 I joined Óglaigh Náisiúnta na hÉireann Teoranta (ONET), a support organisation for ex-service personnel of the Irish Defence Services. The organisation began sometime around 1950 and was formed as an amalgam of a number of ex-service-men's organisations which had sprung up after soldiers, sailors and airmen had been demobbed following service during the 'Emergency', known to the rest of the western world as World War Two. Today, ONET's facilities and accommodation have grown from house to houses in three centres in Ireland. The old house, 'Brú na bhFiann' in Smithfield in Dublin's north inner city was demolished during the redevelopment of Smithfield Market area and replaced with a state-of-the-art forty-bedroom complex which was officially opened by the then President of Ireland and Patron of ONET, Mrs. Mary McAleese. The new home contains a reception area, a bar, a kitchen, and a dining room capable of seating up to ninety people as well as a laundry and administration offices. The other two houses are Beechwood House in Letterkenny, Donegal and Custume House in Athlone, County Westmeath. The organisation's patron is the current President of Ireland, Michael D. Higgins. Most of the members of ONET have served overseas, many of them recipients of awards for bravery and distinguished service and many, like me with a story to tell. Others who have no living family or who have fallen on hard times avail of the services and will see out their days in the care of the only family they know – army comrades. Ceremonial parades and wreath-laying ceremonies as well as outings and social events are features of the organisation's activities.

With my penchant for organisation and having had a stellar role in charge of the Men's Club, I could already see areas that could do with some improvement. I made submissions and complained about accounts and the issue of 1916 commemorative medals. Having once again assumed that with membership would automatically come an entitlement to take them to task, I complained to the Board about spending. But all I have succeeded in doing is dirtying my bib with ONET. Friends insist that the money is well spent; homeless men are finding shelter and solace, where medical care is also provided, and their needs taken care of. I laud the work, but I had always been of the opinion that those in charge should be doing this work on a voluntary basis.

I have also taken the Association of Retired Commissioned Officers to task on a number of issues. My friends try to convince me that there are two sides to every story but only one reveals itself to me. The wife of a couple I've known and loved for over forty years calls me 'an eejit' and we laugh. Sometimes I think I am making progress, that I am slowly freeing myself and slowly rising above the need to concern myself with matters that have little relevance to my personal life. But then, something else irritates me and I'm off again, digging up whatever evidence of some misdemeanour or a remark made that didn't sit well with me. One minute I am jovial, the next minute I am swamped in venom.

In the past, I put it all down to groupthink. I devoured the work of psychologist, Irving Janis who wrote extensively on groupthink and its effect on the individual and on the group. According to Janis, one of the eight symptoms is 'direct pressure on dissenters' – members are under pressure not to express arguments against any of the group's views. What stood out was the observation that a group is especially vulnerable to groupthink when its members are similar in background. Arthur Meier Schlesinger Junior who was part of the Kennedy Administration and who was in the operations room when the 'Bay of Pigs' operation was being planned wrote in his memoir of the Kennedy administration, *A Thousand Days:*

Kennedy in the White House, 'The president wanted a unanimous decision so I bitterly reproached myself for having remained silent during these crucial discussions,' he said. The book won him his second Pulitzer Prize in 1965.

I had been part of an organisation whose hallmark was group-think: I had been trained to fight as part of an army; to kill an enemy on behalf of the group. It was familiar territory. At the same time, with the exception of short periods throughout my military career, I seldom felt part of a working environment and with the exception of my trips to opera performances, my social life has been deficient, to say the least. Groups scared me and yet it was in groups that I tried to find social connection and a sense of fraternity. I continued to be deeply depressed. At times I fought the urge to kill myself to rid my family of the 'moody one' and to rid myself of pain, all the while traipsing in and out of hospitals and doctors' consulting rooms as my physical health deteriorated.

CHAPTER 8

Implacable Rage

I am not the man I was meant to be.
My soul was taken by a beast I try to forgive,
who left me in this hell where I continue to writhe.
This is my testament to the walls of Jerusalem-
I was nineteen when the Hosannas ended!

Jerusalem, Michael J. Whelan

I read somewhere that we learn about the evils of the world in many ways but when it happens through a violent act, it leaves us broken and afraid. From then on, we learn to armour ourselves – not just against such inhuman treatment but against all human engagement – by adopting attitudes and behaviours that we believe will protect us. We believe that our innocence and trust and kindness render us vulnerable and exploitable and we vow to prevent it happening again. But beneath the thin layer of independence our lives are plagued by unmet needs, unrealised potential and a feeling of perpetual loss, living in a state of quiet desperation that can often erupt into a wild, implacable rage.

Following Jerusalem, I withdrew from the rest of humanity. My heart problems worsened and following a Cather ablation in 2013, I awoke from the anaesthetic bursting with so much energy that I thought my body would explode. For two weeks I wanted to climb walls. No longer able to run like I did in the past, I became more and more agitated. Unable to contain this gut-wrenching agitation, I opened my laptop that was sitting on top of the piano and started writing. What fell onto the screen was a stream of consciousness, spilling my guts, rambling through the hellish highlights of over fifty years of a broken life which began in Jerusalem in 1965. As I wrote, the injustices that I had suffered at the hands the defence forces and the Irish State began to take on even bigger proportions. My feeling that it had been me against the world all along grew into ferocious rage and became so profoundly embedded in my mind that I couldn't see the wood for the trees. I didn't even read what I had written. Each time I was gripped by anger I just kept adding more and more.

Three years later, in 2016, while I was waiting for a flight at the airport in Munich the Pensions Board's decision to reduce my benefit took on a more disturbing hue. The previous evening, I had been going through old papers. The full realisation that Army Pensions Administration, Finance Branch, Department of Defence, Galway, in rejecting the determination of the Army Pensions Board had appeared to have contrived with medical personnel to reverse the award. The psychiatrist gave the trainee in the Defence Forces exactly what was wanted. It was when I read the statement, a mere assumption on his part, disregarding the opinion of other, eminent professionals – that my 'condition had pre-existed enlistment' that the full impact hit me. I was appalled at what I read. The Department of Defence wasn't accepting PTSD under any circumstances and even in the final report, it refused to accept the case by arguing that my decision to plead PTSD in the beginning was my undoing. I came to the conclusion that at the very least, the Administrator refused to believe that I had been raped in 1965. In hindsight, perhaps he could be forgiven. His difficulty in believing my story could be viewed as justifiable – due to lack of evidence. Perhaps I should have tried to track down the corporal who had been seen me in the aftermath of the attack in Jerusalem. He might have described the circumstances of the morning after the assault and the state of distress that I was in. The corporal, now deceased, was the only person – other than my assailant – within the forces who knew what happened to me: the nearest I had to a witness.

The Administrator stated that the 'allegation' that I was the victim of a sexual assault was in question. His statement read:

> 'It was not developed or investigated further by the examining medical team. The alleged assault occurred not while on duty but on leave from UNFICYP in Jerusalem. Thus, the admissibility or otherwise of this aspect of his claim *is open to serious doubts*'.

He did not accept that the nature of my condition (PTSD and its attendant complications) was attributable to my service with the defence forces. He concluded by casting aspersions, even on my position with the Air Corps as a civilian:

> 'It is also significant that Captain McQuaid has, of his own volition chosen to re-enter a military environment by virtue of his employment as a civilian storeman with the Air Corps at Baldonnel,' he said.

I would be interested to know what he would have done had he spent over a year looking for work in a myriad of other companies and organisations without success, trying to match his skills and abilities with anything that was on offer. Or if he had any idea of the pain and frustration of rejection. Of course, I was not given the chance to explain that it had been a gesture of goodwill on the part of former colleagues that had enabled me to find a position with the Irish Air Corps. Civilian organisations and companies were not interested. I did not realise it at the time but in hindsight, the Air Corps was exactly where I needed to be – among peers: people who knew and understood my military past, who spoke the same language and who knew instinctively the need for me to be gainfully occupied. As soldiers, we were well used to turning our hands to anything and they knew that time to ruminate was not good. They had kept me sane.

When I returned from overseas duty with the United Nations in 1967/68 I had no academic qualifications. I came home to a country that was under a dark cloud of economic recession and employment opportunities were about as plentiful as hens' teeth. The state of Ireland's economy and the scarcity of jobs, even for people with third level qualifications was well known. When the American Globemasters and Hercules troop carriers were flying across the Irish Sea, laden with young Irish soldiers on their way to the Congo, Ireland was still exporting emigrants as it had been for decades. Most of these emigrants had traditionally been of the unskilled variety, destined for hard, manual labour at their final destination. But unlike previous decades, they now were joined by third level college graduates bound for America, Australia and England. As emigration and unemployment levels reached their peak, the loss of these academics, one of Ireland's few prized assets at the time, was commonly referred to as the 'brain drain'. The Administrator did not seem to take into consideration that despite everything, I still had strong connections to and a great affinity with the people with whom I had served. After all, the Defence Forces had been my life and I had missed it more than I realised. The job at Baldonnel had been a life-saver for which I will be forever grateful.

Eventually the personnel of the Army Pensions Board changed and in time, a second Board was set up before which I was required to attend – without being furnished with any of their deliberations to date. This was the subject of an application for Judicial Review which was granted by the late Mr. Justice Robert Barr of the High Court. A third Board was not convened so I was denied the opportunity to speak directly to an 'Army Pensions Board Mark 3'. When I read this correspondence on the night before travelling to Munich my heart sank to the floor. The report made me look like a liar, someone who was chancing his arm. As a soldier who had a long and impeccable service record, who was a stickler for duty and performance to the highest standard, I was seething with anger at all of this. I was also angry at myself for having submitted myself to examination after examination and for throwing myself at the mercy of this organisation, which amounted to nothing more than an insurance company with only one aim – to make it as difficult as possible for claimants to receive their rightful dues. I am convinced that the Administrators of my case – two civil servants – have many questions to answer.

I learned recently of a soldier who was discharged from the army because he was 'physically unfit'. In fact, he was as fit as a fiddle, physically. He suffered from seizures, but the army medics refused to acknowledge his condition – in case he applied for a disability pension! Thankfully, having been properly diagnosed elsewhere, he succeeded in obtaining his rightful dues. His condition was, in all probability due to PTSD. I am adamant that the Disability Pension Scheme needs serious review. The Department of Defence Pensions Administration is usurping the role of the Army Pensions Board and its process of assessment is adversarial. Once the APB makes a determination the applicant should be informed immediately and not left waiting for years for a decision by the Minister. There is an urgent need for a judicial inquiry into the role of Defence is this regard. My case borders on the criminal – taking nine years, three rejections and a judicial review. It beggars belief. All of this is due to the invisibility of what Carl Jung refers to as 'psychic wounds' – wounds that are carried in the mind. I looked reasonably normal on the outside; inside, I was bleeding to death.

About two years ago I had a long chat with a social worker in the defence forces. I told him everything. He is not a medical officer nor a clinical psychologist, but he is a good listener. When he heard the symptoms of PTSD from which I suffered and the various drugs that I had been prescribed for depression and anxiety, he told me that he had been speaking with a soldier's wife earlier in the year who told him that all she wanted was her husband back. She said that her husband was not the person that he was before he was given the anti-malaria drug, Lariam before he went overseas, with the UN. Since then, he has become a different person. She was hoping that he will not become violent; if he does she will have to leave him and take the children with her. That family will have a long, painful journey on the road to a) recognition of his condition and b) a hard battle for redress. This woman attributes her husband's condition to Lariam, the drug offered to prevent Malaria. We agreed that some people's systems can handle drugs; for others, they can have devastating effects. I told the social worker that I suspected that as a veteran of service overseas, the man was probably also suffering from PTSD. The effects of drugs, compounded by PTSD, can screw up a person's mind for the remainder of his or her life.

I knew of a former soldier from Dublin who was given Lariam when he served with the Irish army in Liberia and Chad in 2007. He has said publicly that he still feels side effects like suicidal ideation and depression and he thinks that the Irish Defence Minister should order an inquiry and designate professional people to help those suffering from the side effects of Lariam. The General Secretary of The Permanent Defence Force Other Ranks Association (PDFORRA), Gerry Rooney says that Ireland should follow UN advice which recommends that alternative drugs should be used for soldiers who suffer from the drug's side-effects. Alternatives are given when people are deployed for very short periods of time, but the tendency is to prescribe Lariam for soldiers going on full missions. Rooney also said that the Irish Defence Forces are continuing to use Lariam, based on the findings of a specialist working group which deemed it to be the 'most effective anti-malaria drug', particularly on missions where, due to conflict, supply links to medication may be disrupted.

In 2013 the specialist working group investigated all the various issues surrounding the use of Lariam and obtained advice from leading medical experts. Those experts concurred with the practices followed by the defence forces in prescribing Lariam. The working group has spent years examining developments in the context of the defence forces' use of malaria chemoprophylaxis – examining updated patient safety information, changes to product character-istics, changes in product licensing/authorisation and identification of any new anti-malarial medications on the market. In this regard it has sought any national and international expert advice on the use of malaria chemoprophylaxis and its usage in other countries' armed forces. PDFORRA has been engaged in discussions regard-ing the appropriate anti-malaria drug that should be issued and the question of side effects from taking Lariam has been a constant feature of these lengthy discussions.

During the 1960s and 1970s huge resources were poured into anti-malarial research. The Experimental Therapeutics Division of the Walter Reed Army Institute of Research in Washington D.C. developed Mefloquine in 1970. Coded number WR 431,000, it was one of over five hundred thousand chemical compounds inves-tigated by the United States Armed Forces to treat the consequences of malaria in Vietnam. When the war in Vietnam ended the United States Armed Forces handed over the formula to Roche Pharmaceu-ticals who subsequently manufactured Mefloquine – now brand-named, Lariam – commercially for the tourist industry. But there have been problems with Lariam since then and various interna-tional agencies which perform global drug surveillance have issued findings of serious side-effects that people have experienced since taking the drug. As a result of their findings the World Health Organisation issued warnings around its use in 1992. The United Nations banned the use of Lariam for their armed forces during the war in Cambodia. In 1995 the Civil Aviation Authority banned its use by flight crew members. But in spite of the growing mass of evidence against Lariam as well as the proactive responses of some organisations, it took another six years before any serious attempt was made to scientifically evaluate the clinical side-effects of this drug. The first randomised controlled trial on Lariam was not performed until 2001 by which time it had been administered on a consistent basis to the armed forces. Before then, it had been on sale to the public for over ten years.

I found the results of the trials quite startling. Neuropsychiatric disturbances along with cardiovascular problems such as arrhythmias were found and there are now several recorded cases of sudden death associated with Lariam – apart from suicide. I began to wonder if I had been sensitive to – or had in any way been affected by the cocktail of tablets and inoculations that I had received before my overseas missions. During the early 1960s, daily Proguanil Prophylaxis, coupled with anti-mosquito measures were given to soldiers to control malaria during overseas deployments. Certainly, anti-malaria drugs were administered to our soldiers on the first overseas mission to the Congo in 1960 and before every mission since then. But the drug branded Lariam was not prescribed to Irish soldiers until deployment on the mission to Eritrea in 2001, therefore, I doubt if I was given Lariam for my tour of duty in Lebanon in 1980. But given the growing list of health issues that have arisen since then I am beginning to wonder if the anti-malaria drugs that we were given at that time were similar in chemical composition to Larium.

In the summer of 2016 the then Minister for Defence, Simon Coveney told the Irish Parliament that the working group had been recently reconvened and asked to provide an updated report to him later in the year. Was it a coincidence that at the same time as the Minister's announcement there was an announcement made by Roche Pharmaceuticals confirming that from July 31st, 2016 the drug would no longer be sold in Ireland? Roche Pharmaceuticals is being sued by Irishman Andrew Bryce who claims that side-effects – including panic attacks and dizziness – he experienced after taking the drug on his honeymoon have ruined his life. The Defence Forces is also facing a tranche of legal claims from former soldiers who took Lariam before overseas missions. A spokesperson for Roche said that the move to withdraw Lariam from the Irish market was 'a commercial decision' and not linked to any legal or safety issue. Well, Roche would say that, wouldn't they? Roche also said that Ireland was the only country where the drug was being withdrawn. But despite concerns over its safety, the Department of Defence has stood over its use by the defence forces and the defence forces will continue to be able to buy the drug from international wholesalers – at least for the time being.

From unit records I have learned that the drug issued to soldiers with the 2nd Infantry Group, ONUC was Darachlor (Pyrimethamine). Interestingly a doctor also saw fit to report that the altitude at which they would be serving was 5,000 feet so acclimatisation would be slow, particularly for those over forty – and could cause chest issues. He also mentioned that canvas was an unsuitable form of accommodation in the tropics – completely contra indicated. Fortunately, most of us were young and fit and while I was in the Congo I was too busy enjoying the adventure. However, I did come down with some form of what was diagnosed as 'flu and I was in the care of the medics for about a week.

No-one will ever know the extent of drug related problems among soldiers and we will never know how many cases of Post-Traumatic Stress Disorder, (or Gulf War Syndrome among U.S. troops) were triggered by the effects of Lariam. There could be hundreds of thousands. Meanwhile healthy young men, many of them former soldiers from across the world, have been jumping off cliffs or shooting or stabbing themselves and/or their wives and families to death. Lariam aside, PTSD alone could have this effect. PTSD brought me close to disaster. From my many 'near misses' – coming close to shooting subordinates, fellow officers and employers and on the brink of killing myself – I can empathise.

I told the social worker that in my opinion, the woman's husband had 'died' overseas. By the time the side-effects from the drug had manifested it was already too late. Here was a man who may have been at risk prior to this and the failure of the army medical professionals to detect that risk is an example of the lack of training given to these doctors – even the psychiatrists – whose knowledge has been limited to classic symptoms of 'abnormal psychology'. Medical professionals in this country are only beginning to scratch the surface as regards PTSD. These people are employed by an organisation – the Military – that on a daily basis exposes its soldiers to trauma, to fear and to physical danger. The very nature of a soldier's role involves prolonged periods of physical and mental challenge – both at home and especially in war zones overseas. Peacekeeping is not about swaggering into some wild west saloon, firing a few shots in the air and hollering, "Come on now, lads. Cut out the fighting!" The effects of exposure to the horrors of armed conflict may not manifest immediately. They could take months – maybe years – to manifest after exposure to those events. Post-traumatic stress from combat, unprovoked attack, or the trauma of scraping up the bodies of people – including children – tortured or blown to pieces in some godforsaken war zone is enough to haunt a soldier for the rest of his or her life. Many soldiers will have died overseas – not physically, but in heart and soul and mind. Right now, there are countless numbers of former Irish soldiers living in hostels, roaming the streets of cities throughout Ireland and in the U.K., hopeless and homeless – and deeply traumatised. Overseas service can – and does – cause change. Trauma causes damage, much of it in the form of deep, unseen wounds. The addition of a drug that alters their gut and brain chemistry, turning them into lunatics, will impact on them and their families for generations to come. And the saddest part will be the futile search for justice from the organisation – and the country – to which they have given their all.

The failure to debrief soldiers after a mission can lead to serious problems, among them alcoholism and illegal drug abuse. It is my belief that each unit returning from a mission should be re-formed after a couple of weeks' leave and brought back together for at least three weeks during which problems can be re-worked and counselling provided if necessary. Acknowledging that drugs can affect cognitive functioning and compound the symptoms of PTSD is vital. We need a counselling programme in situ, provided by people who are trained psychotherapists and not simply well-meaning listeners. Of the forty-seven Irish troops who died in Lebanon some of them were suicides and some at the hands of deranged fellow soldiers. Literally thousands more have come home suffering from physical and psychological damage, leading to alcoholism, relationship and family break ups, aloneness and alienation.

In the United States, PTSD is recognised and published in a DSM Manual. In Britain and Ireland, saving the State costs at the expense of the individual has taken precedent over acknowledgement, investigation and treatment. Therapy has been limited, hitherto delivered through Personnel Support Services, (PSS), a mix of social workers, headed up by a non-professional – i.e. a non-medically trained person. In 2016, the Organisation of Ex-Servicemen (ONET) and the IUNVA signed off on an agreement with the Department of Defence that soldiers in therapy would be given six sessions of counselling therapy, post discharge. Both organisations are grant-aided by the Department of Defence and recognised in the White Paper on Defence, Section 7 – 'Veterans' Policy'. This agreement might be a move in the right direction, but it is by no means enough.

In the final analysis it is easy to understand the traumatic after effects of war. It is easy to understand that drugs can have devastating side-effects. What I still find hard to deal with is the fact that it was the actions of my own countrymen – most of them in positions of some seniority and authority – that led to my torment. No member of the defence forces has acknowledged this. On the contrary, the defence forces, through the Army Pensions Administration have denied it. And not only denied it but they have gone to extreme lengths to avoid responsibility – by refusing to acknowledge even the possibility of having a criminal in their employ and acknowledging that sexual assault can – and does – result in full-blown PTSD. Nor was there any effort to help me to recover; no offer of treatment. In 1965, my NCO saw me in deep distress but could offer no treatment and no comfort. In today's world, a rape victim is treated in a clinic or a hospital for his or her injuries, probably given pain killing drugs and maybe tranquilisers and offered counselling. I was left on my own to deal with it and in later life, to find doctors and therapists and pay for my treatment, like any private citizen. Psychiatrists agree that if sufferers from PTSD are not treated at the early stage, it will affect the rest of their lives.

The 'package' on offer to an enlisted soldier consists of a few of basic meals a day, a uniform, a bed, a weapon and as small a wage as the defence forces can get away with. If the soldier survives a mission, he/she has a medal pinned to their chest. Soldiers, especially foot soldiers are dispensable. It is only in old age that this realisation dawns and they are left with the memories. Few of them will ever speak, for if they speak, no-one will understand. The traumas arise in the dead of night: strangled cries echoing around the rooms, some empty, some occupied by family members who have been warned to 'just put it down to bad dreams' because sometimes it's better to leave everything unsaid; sometimes there is comfort to be found in the ignorance of loved ones.

When I joined the Defence Forces in 1963, most of my fellow recruits were – like me – teenagers. But while I grew up in a loving family home with impeccable moral standards and received a good, basic education, a large proportion of others had been incarcerated in the infamous industrial schools where they suffered the unspeakable brutality of so-called 'Christian' brothers and priests, brutality that included repeated beatings, sexual assault – and rape. By the time they enlisted, they were either already weakened and vulnerable, easy pickings for sexual predators or they themselves had become predators. I discovered as recently as the summer of 2018 that it was well known that some men were 'at it'. My informant told me that he knew of one victim who made a complaint and the perpetrator was court martialled. I never knew any of this and now wondered if, all through my career I had been living in a bubble.

CHAPTER 9

The Reality of PTSD

*There are no palms for my feet to walk upon
in the souks and the aromas of this city
and in the places where I pray.*

Jerusalem, Michael J. Whelan

My prayers for my mother's recovery from septicaemia in 1997 went unanswered. With her death came the end of a long list of unanswered prayers and the annihilation of my faith in God, in the afterlife, in saints, angels, rituals and any philosophy preached by the Catholic Church. On the plus side I had achieved my dream of becoming a soldier and going to the Congo, but in doing so I had put my mother through a lot of anxiety; her only consolation, after several peacekeeping missions overseas being my return home, still alive. I don't know if she, like the friend who advised me to apply for a disability pension could see that I had changed. If she did, she said nothing. If she didn't it meant that I had maintained a good camouflage. I am sure that among other things, she often wondered why I had never married and settled down and wondered why I was moody and withdrawn a lot of the time.

By this time blind faith had been replaced by a quest for more scientific answers to the questions that plagued my mind and some sort of anaesthesia that might numb the pain of bereavement that was now piled on top of the painful memory of Jerusalem and the thoughts of killing and self-harm. For the most part I had been challenged and gainfully occupied during my years in college – despite bouts of depression. My degree had also been the catalyst for

113

my recommendation for commissioning. But I still felt isolated – even more isolated after my mother died. Although she appeared to know nothing of my torment, she had been there, and her presence was often enough.

Despite my lack of faith, I had considered my rise through the ranks to officer grade in the army to have been a miracle – because I could find no other word with which I could name my good fortune. I had hoped that my achievements would put me on a par with the best of them and that I would retire in comfort, cascading with braids and medals and a glowing record of service. To a large extent that dream was fulfilled. I graduated from two college courses with degrees and I was a commissioned officer, all achieved without the benefit of prayer or any other form of spiritual intercession, on my part.

While studying psychology I was obliged to read and as well as the course material I devoured material outside the curriculum – Descartes, Socrates, Plato and other philosophers. I had to study the works and experiments and case studies of Mesmer, Freud and Jung and learn symptoms of dysfunction in the individual, both behavioural and psychological. But in my experience with both military and civilian medical professionals I had found large differences in treatment and in the handling of health issues between the two. With few exceptions, general practitioners and consultants in the civilian world focus on the welfare of the patient but in military medicine the doctor has a duty of care to both the patient and to the defence forces, as opposed to being entirely an advocate for the patient. Due to the sensitive nature of the subject and its associated stigma, psychiatric illness is a particularly heavy burden on military doctors. From sources within the defence forces I gather that the psychiatric cases presenting in the military psychiatric unit today range from depression and suicidality to addiction. In all cases, whether physical or psychological, the doctor has a duty to also be an advocate for the defence forces. His/her reporting and grading of the individual will naturally result in the determination of eligibility for promotions, renewal of contracts and the ability of the soldier to serve on overseas missions.

As I began to unravel some of the questions regarding my own medical record, having presented with boils, pneumonia, pleurisy and shingles and prone to hypertension, I was amazed by the nonchalance with which the doctor in St. Bricin's had deemed me 'cured' and fit for another overseas mission to Cyprus. Did it not occur to any of the doctors that after each overseas mission I had presented with some sickness? This should have alerted them to the possibility of an underlying cause, like a computer virus that will eventually cause the machine to crash, or completely wipe every piece of information from the hard drive. But with copious medical notes that charted my growing number of ailments, nothing unusual was detected. I was also mentally ill, but no-one noticed. Nor was I able to confide in anyone.

Unless there have been radical changes in army medical practice since I was a soldier, huge oversights in people's physical, emotional and mental health still allow serving members of the defence forces to fall through the cracks, especially those like me – enlisted soldiers who may not have the courage or the vocabulary to voice their need for intervention, who try to maintain the stance of the 'hard man' or 'tough woman' to save face – and to hold onto a secure job. It then falls to a discerning friend, a fellow soldier or a family member to notice that all is not as it should be and to pick up the pieces. At any rate, by the time I retired from the Air Corps job I had lost all faith in the medical arm of the Irish Defence Forces.

During my first episode of depersonalisation I had no idea what was happening. As time went on and the episodes occurred again and again, I could not understand why I trundled in and out of black moods – or why I had run into conflict, again and again with superiors and fellow workers when all I was trying to do was my best. I could eventually work out that the stress of conflict, the proximity to conflict and an episode of depersonalisation were connected, simply by the realisation that one was followed almost immediately by the other. But as the incidents increased I could not understand why an episode could engulf me, even without obvious external stimulus – and without warning. Then I noticed that even when reading the newspapers or watching news items on television – especially those about what are referred to as 'hot spots' ravaged by conflict – the more tormented I became. I also suffered an attack while attending an opera abroad and it was only then that I began to suspect that even in that heightened state of euphoria, elicited by the beauty and magnificence of the music, I could be susceptible to a panic attack!

I didn't stop watching the News. Instead I devoured philosophy and tried to grapple with psychology. In the course of study – and from personal experience – I began to see how stress, which could be positive or negative could trigger physical symptoms. I also discovered – more through trial and error than through study – that highly charged emotion, mostly anger, could lead to a panic attack. This realisation was rather frightening because if this were the case, it reduced my chances of controlling it. Slowly a light was shed on 'conditioning': the 'training' of the human mind beneath the level of conscious awareness. Like Pavlov's dogs I had learned to experience an episode by reacting emotionally – not just to an actual stressful event like an argument but a word, a sound, a piece of music, a smell, a memory or even a fleeting thought could spark an attack.

My modus operandi had become one of defence. It is only in later years that I have begun to understand that my behaviour had at times seemed irrational and incomprehensible to those with whom I worked. This was revealed in a statement by a fellow officer as part of my application for a disability pension. Captain J. Burns and I had served in the 1st Cavalry Squadron and we had maintained contact during my service in both the Military College and in the QMG's branch and beyond. He stated that he was aware that I was under 'considerable personal emotional strain which affected my relationship with both friends and colleagues, that I appeared to be unsettled in any environment and suffered frequent mood swings'. He went on to say that 'this personal strain seemed to peak in 1989 and that it was obvious to most observers that I was extremely upset – even to the extent that I could barely hold a conversation with friends and acquaintances. Subsequently, I still found it difficult to settle and had difficulty dealing with *any* stress and even in some cases, *the normal strains of everyday life*'. At the time I read this, all of what he said went over my head. Looking back many years later, that statement alone convinced me that I was an emotional and psychological mess: someone who should have been retired on medical grounds. The more I learned about the psychology of stress, the more I wondered, given that I had a mental condition, how I had survived at all since the age of nineteen!

Recently, a memory surfaced: I was only eighteen when, in September 1963 I had been sent with a corporal and two other young soldiers to St. Bricin's Military Hospital in Dublin to provide a guard for a soldier being held in Ward 5, known colloquially as 'the rubber room'. Rather bizarrely, we were armed with bayonets for our own protection. We didn't have any specific training for this task, apart from a short briefing given to us by a staff nurse when we arrived. She told us that the patient was in bed and had to be guarded until the next day when he would to be taken under escort to Carlow Psychiatric Hospital. We settled in. After tea, the patient, who was a very tall man got out of bed and headed for the smallest soldier in our group and threatened him with a razor blade. We called a nurse and she persuaded him to return to bed. Later, he was at it again! This time the young soldier, who was on the Eastern Command boxing team, flattened him with a punch to the jaw. All hell broke out; nurses everywhere! We were dismissed. I don't know if that unfortunate patient had served on any of the earlier missions in the Congo, but I now believe that he was probably in the throes of PTSD – or what was in those days called 'shellshock'.

Contrary to the media reports emanating from the Army Press Office in the period following the later missions in Lebanon, the Army's understanding of PTSD was still a long way off. One newspaper headline screamed, 'The Army says the incidence of post-traumatic stress disorder is miniscule'. The article stated that 'according to the director of the Army Medical Services, Col. Michael Walsh, the incidence of PTSD is so miniscule that it would be invidious to give the actual number. And to the best of the army's knowledge, Private Seán Courtney is the first soldier suffering from PTSD to be involved in a serious criminal incident'.

Courtney had bludgeoned a young woman to death in the Dublin Mountains in 1991. He had served two tours of duty in South Lebanon. His first tour of duty in 1987 was uneventful but on the second in 1988, an Israeli tank had opened fire over his unit's observation post. He had also had a gun pointed at him at a checkpoint and in his trial, gave evidence of an incident in which his friend had committed suicide, shooting himself in a toilet cubicle. Courtney had found his friend's body in a pool of blood.

An Israeli tank firing indiscriminately, with deadly intent, over an observation post in the mayhem that was Lebanon is not the same as heavy artillery shelling aimed at mapped out targets under controlled conditions and a couple of military Fouga jets flying low over troops hiding in the bushes and the bog-holes in the Glen of Imaal! Courtney's experiences were enough to 'qualify' him for enough PTSD criteria to have been taken into proper counselling and discharged on medical grounds. I was surprised that Courtney hadn't died from shock when he found his friend on the floor of a toilet with his brains blown out.

Courtney, who had served in the army for six years told detectives that he had undergone psychiatric treatment for stress at St Bricin's Military Hospital after this incident. I don't know if he was discharged with a clean bill of mental health – deemed 'cured'. After these experiences he began drinking heavily, he cried regularly and had nightmares. I'm not sure if the question of anti-Malaria drugs was mentioned during his trial. At any rate his marriage broke up. His Counsel said that Courtney was, 'at the time he killed thirty-two-year-old Patricia O'Toole, for all practical purposes, insane' The Gárdaí and the Court didn't believe him. The jury rejected the defence motion to find him not guilty by reason of insanity and after a six-hour deliberation he was found guilty by a majority of ten to two, convicted of murder and sentenced to fifteen years in prison. While Courtney may have had violent tendencies before enlistment, this account doesn't say much for the psychiatric assessment procedure or the 'psychiatric treatment' at St. Bricin's! That Courtney slipped through the cracks and ended up taking his alcohol-fuelled anger out on a defenceless woman in the Dublin Mountains was an unfortunate occurrence – and just that. Medical negligence – ignorance, really – would never be acknowledged.

There are uncanny echoes of the court's disbelief of Courtney's evidence and its rejection of his plea of insanity – temporary or otherwise – in the Army Pensions Board's rejection of my claim for a disability pension. One of the reasons cited by the medical examiners was 'failure to fill the criteria for complete PTSD'. Given the lack of understanding and the denial of the extent of PTSD by the director of medical services, it is small wonder that my disability pension was reduced, and I doubt that the Diagnostic and Statistical Manual of Mental Disorders (DSM) was used to reach this conclusion.

The manual called the DSM was created in the United States to guide medical practitioners in their understanding and treatment of PTSD. There are clusters of symptoms outlined in this manual and when I read it, I found that I was reading my own medical history. The specifying and qualifying experiences of traumatic events that should be met to meet the requirements for a diagnosis of PTSD – four sets of 'symptom clusters' and two subtypes and the requirements for meeting these criteria around the duration of symptoms and how these symptoms impact on one's functioning – ruling out substance use and medical illnesses are proof enough that PTSD is a genuine and unquestionable condition and that I met all of the criteria.

Examples include 'Criterion A: Traumatic event'. To meet Criterion A, trauma survivors must have been exposed to actual or threatened death, serious injury or sexual violence. The exposure can be direct, witnessed or indirect – i.e. simply by hearing of a relative or close friend who has experienced the event. Indirectly experienced death must be 'accidental or violent, repeated or extreme'. (I'm not quite sure if I am reading this correctly; how can death be 'repeated'?). It also includes indirect exposure to qualifying events, usually by professionals, discounting non-professional exposure by media. I gather that this convoluted statement means that even watching an amateur video of a violent event can trigger PTSD – just as I found that watching the News was enough to set off an episode of depersonalisation.

I wasn't simply 'exposed to' sexual violence but I actually experienced – suffered sexual violence – in Jerusalem and I came face to face with the threat of death in Lebanon. I certainly ticked that box! Criterion A should have summed it up for the army medical examiners and resulted in an open and shut case, no further questions asked. It didn't.

According to the DSM there are classifications among clinicians who work in trauma between 'Big T-traumas,' such as those listed above and 'Little-t traumas'. Little-t traumas can include complicated grief, divorce, non-professional media exposure to trauma or childhood emotional abuse. Psychiatry recognises that these can result in post-traumatic stress, even if they don't qualify for the PTSD diagnosis.

My 'complicated grief' covered many aspects of my life both at home and overseas. I grieved for the brutality of my loss of innocence, I grieved for the boy that once was, I grieved for the loss of my strength, for the loss of my soul, my ability to grow and I grieved for the loss of my manhood. According to the DSM there is no longer a requirement for someone to have had an intense emotional response at the time of the event. It is now recognised that the emotional response can take a long time to appear. Many military veterans and sexual assault survivors had previously been excluded and denied treatment because it was only years later that they began to show signs of PTSD. This proves that the incidences of soldiers killing, self-harming or committing suicide <u>months or years</u> after a traumatic event *is finally recognised as PTSD.*

Under Criterion B: 'Intrusion or Re-experiencing', symptoms envelope ways that someone re-experiences the event. This could be intrusive thoughts or memories, nightmares related to the traumatic event, flashbacks: feeling like the event is happening again, psychological and physical reactivity to reminders of the traumatic event. Even the date of an anniversary. Intrusive thoughts, memories, nightmares and flashbacks have formed the tapestry of my life since 1965. Another box ticked.

Criterion C is categorised by 'Avoidant symptoms': ways that sufferers may try to avoid memories of the event. It must include avoiding thoughts or feelings connected to the traumatic event or avoiding people or situations connected to the traumatic event. My avoidant symptoms would secure a little golden statuette at the Oscars! The problem was they couldn't be sustained; I couldn't fool myself all of the time. All too often I plummeted into depression. I was often so consumed by anger and frustration I was unable to function.

Criterion D: 'negative alterations in mood or cognitions' is new. It has taken a long time for psychiatrists to realise that many symptoms that have long been manifest in PTSD sufferers include a decline in someone's mood or thought patterns, which can include memory problems that are exclusive to the event, negative thoughts or beliefs about one's self or the world, a distorted sense of blame on one's self – or others who are related to the event – being stuck in severe emotions related to the trauma (e.g. horror, shame, sadness), severely reduced interest in pre-trauma activities or feeling detached, isolated or disconnected from other people. It seems to me that none of the symptoms in this category existed or if they did, were not properly considered by the Army Pensions Board in 1993. Horror, shame, sadness, reduced interest in pre-trauma activities. Feeling detached, isolated and disconnected from other people – these too have been woven into my life's tapestry and continue, albeit to a lesser degree, to this day.

Criterion E – increased arousal symptoms – is a term used to describe the ways that the brain remains 'on edge', wary and watchful of further threats. Symptoms include difficulty concentrating, irritability, increased temper or anger, difficulty falling or staying asleep, hypervigilance or being easily startled. Criterion E describes my state from 1965 to 1993 to a T. Yet, it was glossed over in my medical reports.

Criteria F, G and H: all of these describe the severity of the symptoms listed above. Basically, they have to have lasted for at least a month. They must seriously affect one's ability to function and they can't be due to substance use, medical illness or anything except the event itself. After Jerusalem they lasted for many years – and intensified after my life was threatened in Lebanon.

Finally, the 'Subtype': 'Dissociation' – is now significant enough to have, in recent years, been set apart from the symptom clusters. It is now recognised that while there are several types of dissociation, *only two* are included in the DSM: depersonalisation, or feeling disconnected from oneself, derealisation – a sense that one's surroundings aren't real.

I have spent a lifetime trying to deal with both. Game Set and Match!

The DSM has gone through a number of revisions through the years, and recently the 5th edition was released. Post-Traumatic Stress Disorder (PTSD) was one of the diagnosis that received some revisions. Apart from Criterion D – negative alterations in mood or cognitions, which is new – I am not sure how many others existed at the time of the examinations that I had to submit to in 1993. On reading them today it would seem that I presented with every symptom on the list. Perhaps I would have qualified with flying colours had I been assessed in the last few years!

The psychiatrist at St. Bricin's Hospital issued his report on the 29th of November 2000, outlining my medical history and the names of the psychiatric professionals that I had attended of which there were five, only one of whom acknowledged the severity of my symptoms resulting from the incident in Lebanon.

On the other hand, in August 1997, the consultant psychiatrist in Cork had stated that I had developed PTSD 'of considerable significance as a result of the episode in Lebanon' and he felt that my personality had changed. I had told him that my motivation to leave the army was because of the lack of promotional prospects. In my ignorance – or innocence – I was treating this like a job interview rather than a medical examination. The truth was a lot more sinister – the proximity of guns and ammunition! I should have told him that there were times when I came to within a hair's breadth of shooting myself – or shooting someone else. However, despite my reticence, he deduced correctly that the real reason I had left the army was the result of my recent experience which, in his opinion, had changed my personality and my approach to military life. He went on to comment on my time with The Medical Council where he observed that at the end of the first year, problems began to arise in the area of inter-personal relations with others in the Council and that I had difficulty in accepting the opinion of superiors for the solution of problems When the pressure became too much for me to bear I left. He concluded by stating that although I found employment with the air corps, I remained dissatisfied with life and tended to approach most situations in an aggressive manner. At the time of his report I was attending Dr Abbie Lane, a psychiatrist at a south County Dublin stress clinic. In fact, I had been on anti-depressant medication and receiving psychotherapy there for years, but the Board had not requested a report from Dr Lane.

As a young lad of nine or ten I had flattened a school bully with a punch even though he was twice my size. My army training, with emphasis on physical fitness, stamina and physical endurance, day in, day out to build and maintain physical strength and stamina failed me. I was living in a body that had let me down. My voice couldn't call out for help, my legs couldn't run away, and my hands and arms couldn't lash out in self-defence. Nothing in my army training had prepared me for what happened in February 1965. In a flash, I was set upon by a beast and I could do nothing to defend myself. *I am not the man I was meant to be.*

I realise now that the anger I felt was turned inward – at a body that could not protect itself. I hated it. I wanted to rid myself of this body because it had failed me. I was now trapped inside it and it was my greatest enemy. I succeeded in ignoring it and to all intents and purposes it became paraplegic; from the neck down, it grew numb. It had failed in any situation that posed a threat – beginning in Jerusalem – and later, when I dislodged the gear lever in my patrol vehicle in Lebanon. Even in normal circumstances, when meeting someone for the first time, my mouth would become dry and my throat restricted. My brain could not distinguish between a real threat and an imagined threat, 'guarding' me from exposure to any form of meaningful human interaction.

In Jerusalem I was robbed of the ability to develop. The only way to survive was to accept that I would never have a normal relationship or a family of my own. I now have to accept that physically I am in constant need of medical treatment. Even in my studies of psychology I did not come across any reference to the vast array of the effects of trauma on the human system as a whole. At this point – rather late in the day – I am in no doubt that many of my physical problems arose from stored memories of trauma. The human body cannot lie. According to Dr Bessan van der Kolk, an Austrian psychiatrist, the human body 'keeps the score'. Sadly, few medical professionals in this country were willing to explore or acknowledge this, one exception being Dr Ivor Brown who was viewed by some of his peers as 'nuts'.

Thankfully I am not a murderer and I am not criminally insane, but Captain Burns' summation of my condition was a chilling reminder that I could have been a grave danger to myself and to others. Apart from an NCO in Jerusalem, no-one in the army knew what happened to the boy who left Dublin in 1965 full of *joie de vivre* and pride – the Two Star Private with a UN medal and the prospect of a bright future in what had become his place in the world – the Irish Army. None of my family knew. None of my friends knew.

One psychiatric report used terms like 'passive', 'childlike' and 'dependent', 'emotionally immature' and 'non-stable', having 'a querulant type personality', 'a tendency towards being obsessive, aggravated by my ruminations'. My panic disorders had 'settled down' but when they occurred, they were associated with dryness of the mouth, heart palpitations, breathing difficulties and feelings of inability to escape. It said that I tend to ruminate on perceived injustices: someone who, at one level had achieved a lot in life while at an emotional level had failed to progress'. In his recommendations the writer of that report thought it sufficient to acknowledge that despite considerable intelligent abilities, I had been emotionally damaged by two events. His description of that damage could not have been clearer:

'The aggravation of the emotional trauma caused in Jerusalem occurred whilst serving in Lebanon in the role as an Officer with the United Nations. Trauma of this nature can lead to enduring personality change and this, I believe has occurred in Captain McQuaid's situation. It is highly probable that Captain McQuaid *developed injury and personality change, leading to stunted emotional growth secondary to a sexual assault which* occurred to him at nineteen years of age while serving in the Irish Defence Forces'.

It was not enough to persuade the Army Pensions Board of my entitlement to a full disability pension and, by endeavouring to improve my promotional prospects through education and by displaying qualities that enabled me to rise through the ranks, I had not done myself any favours!

When the Irish United Nations Veteran's Association (IUNVA) was being established, I met a clinical psychologist who was interested in 'PTSD'. She didn't do much but did recommend that I see a psychologist in Baggott Street Hospital. He suggested that I see a psychiatrist at St Patricks Hospital. I attended him for a few months but felt I was getting nowhere. Eventually, I attended Dr. Abbie Lane, a psychiatrist at St John of God's Stress Clinic. After a few months, Dr. Lane knew the whole story. The counselling sessions with Dr Lane helped me to understand to some extent what was going on. I was prescribed drugs which I took for a time but stopped because they were not helping. A few years ago, I was referred to a psychologist in Blackrock. We didn't bond; I didn't like him, mainly because he wanted to 'start at the beginning'. I refused. I was interested only in the present. I did not want to revisit old wounds and I stopped attending. I had lost faith – in God and in medicine of all sorts.

CHAPTER 10

Deliverance of Sorts

There is no end to old stories,
And he sees in the sand
The page where his part is written.

No Man's Land, Michael J. Whelan

In 1977, my friend, David Meade and I met for a drink at the Clarence Hotel on the quays in Dublin and then headed to our first opera, *Turandot* at the Gaiety Theatre. David had been on the 3rd Potential Officers Course. He was posted to Cork in the beginning and eventually moved to Naval HQ in Dublin. We had much in common, not least an interest in opera. We both enjoyed the opera and for me, it was the beginning of a lifelong love of live performance. I studied music for six years at the Royal Irish Academy and now and then, I play piano – badly. But friends tell me that I am quite an authority on Wagner! Having become an ardent Wagner follower, I had become affiliated to the Richard Wagner Verband International, the International Association of Wagner Societies and following advice from Dr James Pritchard of the London society I founded The Wagner Society of Ireland by a notice in *The Irish Times* on the 24th of August 2002. It was during the 'Limerick Ring', the acclaimed *Ring* Cycle, *Der Ring des Nibelungen* staged in Limerick in June that I made the decision. Many leading Wagnerian singers including Janice Baird, USA and Germany, Suzanne Murphy from Limerick, Frode Olsen from Norway, Cork soprano Cara O'Sullivan, Canadian Alan Woodrow and Robin Legatte from the Royal Opera House, Covent Garden, performed with the National

Youth Orchestra of Ireland under the baton of Russian conductor Alexander Anissimov. Held at the Concert Hall in University of Limerick, it was only the second complete performance of the marathon Ring Cycle in Ireland. The first was held at the Theatre Royal, Dublin, in 1913. The vast production, consisting of Das Rheingold, Die Walküre, Siegfried and Gotterdammerung cost an estimated €530,000 to stage and involved more than fifteen hours of music. Conductor Alexander Anissimov said that he had done some of his most important creative work in Ireland and that to conduct Wagner's Ring in Ireland was his dream come true. This spurred me into action. I decided to strike while the iron was hot.

There was a good response to my notice in *The Times* and the society took off. I moved fast, and I co-designed the website with the late Stephen O'Gorman, MSC and Irish Air Corps. He loved all things mythological and of course, Sibelius but I couldn't turn his head towards my man, Richard Wagner. As founder and chairman, I attended my first congress in Copenhagen in May 2003. I met Dr Wolfgang Wagner and his wife, Gudrun in Copenhagen. I gave Gudrun my card and followed this up with a letter on gold blocking headed paper with the 'Wagner Society of Ireland' printed in Saint Patrick's Blue with a watermark head of Wagner. Really classy. We applied for tickets for the Bayreuth Festival in 2003 and in 2004 we were allocated forty tickets which was astounding. This practice continued up to 2011 when, after the death of Wolfgang, the system changed and there were no tickets issued to any of the one hundred and thirty-nine affiliated societies. Eventually I was confronted by conflict once again and I stood down from my position of the Wagner Society of Ireland, due to ill health.

As I became less physically active, I found escape – and solace – in music. Part of me was re-born through music. I guess it saved my life. It raised me up to a new level so that even though I have lots of health issues I can be philosophical. Wagner's *Tristan und Isolde* is a work from another world, way ahead of its time in musical construction. Ground breaking, written when the composer's life was in turmoil, he was inspired to put aside his work on *Der Ring des Nibelungen* and begin work on *Tristan und Isolde*. His marriage eventually broke up and he was living in exile in Zurich, but despite penury and his awful skin condition, he built his own theatre with its sunken pit and introduced other innovations some of which are used in cinema even today. He was a master of choral music, a genius of the highest order. He died in Venice in 1883, aged sixty-nine. Through his music I believe that one becomes more open to spirituality. In this regard, I also view Beethoven's *9th Symphony* as sacred, the slow movement brings great music to its absolute zenith. Pure music.

Over the years I escaped to Vienna, to Berlin and other cities to attend opera performances, often for the umpteenth time. I love the music and the visual spectacle on stage and through the music I am transported to a benign sanctuary where I want to remain. The numbers of performances that I have attended must have reached Guinness Book of Records proportions. Such obsession is not shared by my friends in opera circles, most of whom are a lot more selective. But the music soothes my soul and lifts my spirits. I attended my twenty-first *Tristan und Isolde* at the Staatsoper Vienna on Sunday, 12th of March 2017. The principal singers were the Bayreuther Festspiele Team, the world's best. The staging was beautiful, and I had an excellent seat in the front row of a box on Level One. The concluding "Liebestod" (Love/Death) is the most beautiful vocal piece ever written. It was very emotional, and l shed tears. When man is confronted by absolute beauty the reaction is tears.

But even music has been a temporary respite. I probably over-identified with Parsifal, the young man in Wagner's opera who is a 'pure fool' – an innocent, a good man who slowly starts to see the evils in the world and who now perceives the world as a place of unending misery. I arrived at the same conclusion. Unlike Parsifal however, I was not lured into perdition by a 'loathly damsel' or a 'goddess' but defiled by a common-or-garden rapist and unlike Parsifal, I was rebuked, ridiculed and left to stew in my pain. Apart from music, no other pursuit has brought me as much joy and relief. I really believed that I died in Jerusalem and that the rest of my time on this earth had been an unending struggle – and a requiem for my lost self. The 'shell' that is left was simply a robotic actor playing the dual roles of protagonist and antagonist, reacting to the push of buttons – a non-person.

This book wasn't planned. Following the Cather ablation in September 2013, possibly due to my reaction to the general anaesthetic, I found myself back to where I was – psychologically and emotionally in 1980 and the only way I could assuage the anger I felt was to write. The wonderful sisters, Áine and Cáit Skelly at the Rathcoole Business Centre, just outside Dublin helped get the pages into some sort of sequence. When they collated these and added in photographs from my time in the army the idea of a book was taking shape. With what I thought was a story I contacted a self-publishing house, but I got no response. I gave it to Don Lavery who is a former newspaper editor. I felt that he would understand my story as his late father, Captain James Lavery served with the 33rd and the 36th Battalions in the Congo and was awarded a Distinguished Services Medal for his actions during a battle in Kipushi in 1962 where armoured cars under his command fired sixty thousand rounds from their Vickers guns in a battle that lasted a whole day. It was Jim who also found the body of Anthony Browne, the last of the victims of the Niemba ambush two years after the tragedy.

Don didn't mince his words. "To be honest, the manuscript needs to be restructured and re-written," he said. "It badly needs to be subbed extensively. There is too much repetition; at times the sequence is all over the place – too much stream of consciousness instead of just telling the story." Duly chastened, I gave it to a former colleague at Baldonnel, UN Veteran, Military Historian, Writer and Award-Winning Poet, Michael J. Whelan. Michael J. is the Curator of the aviation museum at Baldonnel, having earned himself an M.A. in Military History from the National University, Maynooth. His expertise as well as his experiences while serving as a UN peacekeeper in Lebanon and in Kosovo have led to the publication of a number of books, including two books of poetry which have earned him numerous awards. The latest, *Peacekeeper* published by Doire Press, has achieved glowing reviews.

I have known Michael for over twenty years. He is a friend, a soldier with a big heart and a willingness to help. He is one of a handful of souls who could empathise with my plight and he was keen to help in whatever way he could. But he was in the process of collating and moving heaps of material to Military Archives, which now have a collection of material, heretofore buried in attics, in sheds and down behind furniture, scattered all over Ireland and beyond: forgotten service records, mechanical records, photographs and personal and group memorabilia that would never again have seen the light of day. Such was the amount of material involved that it was deemed necessary to hire four professional archivists to assist Michael who had, up until then gathered and sorted the material and established and run the museum single-handedly. The museum collection was launched at a small ceremony in Baldonnel in the summer of 2016, amid a plethora of other celebratory and commemorative events to mark the centenary of the Easter Rising in Dublin in 1916.

Michael suggested engaging the services of a ghost writer whom he knew. Her initial assessment was similar Don Lavery's. She said there were yawning gaps in the timeline and she had questions – a lot of questions. Initially I found the questioning very challenging. I thought I had described a lot, but I had only alluded to the sordid events in Jerusalem and Lebanon in a casual manner. I could not bring myself to elaborate on them in writing and I could certainly not talk about them! This was the first stumbling block. I thought that what I had written told enough of my story. Yes, there were some typos, capital letters in the wrong places, maybe a few paragraphs needing adjusting. Initially, I could see myself having rows with this woman. But somehow, in a roundabout way we got through our first meeting. She agreed to take on the project and try to structure it into a readable manuscript.

When I received the first draft I wept. The original document, and the few words that I had managed to say in our initial conversation, had been skilfully woven into a coherent narrative. There on the page were the words I could not say, as if she had read my mind! But there were more questions to come and another face-to-face conversation which although somewhat easier for me to handle than the first, was still very difficult. I immediately went home to lie down. Emails flew back and forth and then I grew tired of being asked to supply more narrative here, more detail there. The whole thing irritated me. Anger pervaded every waking hour and sleep became even more erratic. I emailed her and said that I wanted to wrap it up. She seemed to understand. But then I felt guilty. Other memories began to surface. I sent her some more material. I suppose she could have declined to continue but she took up from where she had left off and over the next few months, more memories and more details sprung from the past and I began to feel less fraught and anxious. I was still battling serious health problems but towards the end of the year we had a draft of a story.

I had heard that Declan Power would be taking part in a recording an interview for RTÉ Radio at Smock Alley Theatre in Dublin, I decided to ask Declan if he would have a look at the manuscript. As a career soldier and security and defence analyst, Declan is very familiar with overseas service. The film, *The Siege at Jadotville* which is based on Declan's book of the same name had just been released on Netflix and there was a great buzz in army and in veteran circles, although much of it had escaped me. At Smock Alley, Declan would be talking about his book and his role as a script advisor on the film. His co-participant in the programme would be the famous film-maker, John Boorman whose debut novel had just been published. I had seen Boorman's film, *Excalibur* and was struck by the Wagner music score. And, of course I had enjoyed *Deliverance*, especially the theme music, 'Duelling Banjos'.

I decided to go to the event. But I was now walking with the aid of crutches, following a procedure on my left knee and I was tired and uncomfortable. Attending the event seemed like too much of an effort. Besides, events of this nature would take me out of my depth – into unfamiliar territory, among strangers with whom I still believed I had little in common. I purchased a ticket but on the eve of the event I changed my mind and decided not to attend. However, when morning came I had plucked up courage. That evening, with my draft manuscript tucked under my arm, I ventured forth. When the programme ended I introduced myself to Declan. We had a short, convivial chat. He very kindly agreed to read the draft. I needed a drink and hobbled to the Clarence Hotel, the nearest hostelry serving Guinness and ordered a pint. I took about two swigs and left the rest. I was exhausted, and I wanted to go home and go to bed. I was not optimistic. But within a week Declan come back to me with his assessment. "A very compelling and a fascinating read," he said.

I then realised that the chain of events that had led me this far, beginning with the patient sisters in Rathcoole, then to Don Lavery, to Michael Whelan, to Imelda, the ghost writer, to Declan Power seemed to have been uncannily orchestrated. All of these people were encouraging. They all believed my story. They were all eager to support the process, offering their experience, abilities, guidance and above all, understanding. Along the way, I began to wonder if there had been an invisible hand guiding me to these people – the people that I needed – one step at a time. Maybe there was a God after all? But I was still wary and uncomfortable – unused to these one-to-one interactions that seemed too good to be true. But I was beginning to realise that what had begun in a fit of anger at a system that had treated me unfairly had now been taken out of my hands. Like Parsifal, I had stumbled unknowingly into a rare and mystical world where I would become the focus of attention. And like the young King Arthur who is given the magic sword, Excalibur, I would be handed the Holy Spear, the instrument that, in the right hands, had the power to heal. These people could see what I couldn't see – that I had been handed the gift of a story that had now acquired a somewhat bizarre and challenging life of its own. Whereas I had been spitting fire, my trio of helpers had laser vision that illuminated the dusty, yet priceless fragments, lurking in the shadows.

Don Lavery had advised that I should ditch the reams that I had written about the state of the world. "This is superfluous to your story, he said. "The reader wants to hear YOUR story, your unique experiences and not a summation of the world in chaos," But I was still in fighting mode and didn't want to relinquish any of the work that I had put into it. I wanted the essence of it retained. I was angry at governments around the world, including our own – and I was deeply affected by injustice in all its forms. I had often looked in despair at the world, especially at the futility and the waste of war. Greed, avarice and – as I had witnessed in Lebanon – callous disregard for human life seemed to rule the world and I wanted to make my opinions known. I wanted to express the helplessness that I felt, and I wanted to be taken seriously. I had seen too much. I had suffered too much and I had lost over fifty years of my life to a power machine that, although not at war, seemed at the time to have no regard for me or for soldiers in the field – the very same power machine *within* which I had been destroyed, where I had encountered the real threats to my life and suffered their consequences. I sometimes wondered if the Irish Army's role had been a combat role, would I have gone to war to fight with the army, to feel as if I was doing something useful besides volunteering over and over again in order to escape from myself. Would I have been better off fighting in a war? Then, I realise that a there is little difference; soldiers in a war zone, whether in a peacekeeping role or in combat are 'at war'. But, having signed up on several occasions to serve on peacekeeping missions overseas, had I really grasped the meaning of my role on those missions? Had I achieved anything? Had I contributed anything?

I had purchased Michael Whelan's book, *Peacekeeper* but it had sat amid the pile of books that I had started and never finished. Some of them I dip into now and again, but unless the book is about classical music, I quickly lose interest. I don't know if this is yet another symptom of my condition or if it's due to laziness. It can be a drawback because I often miss information that will come to light later – perhaps in conversation or through hearing an interview with an author on radio or television. When that happens, it reignites my interest and I have to rummage through the abandoned piles of books to find the relevant one and then try to find the information.

When I began to read *Peacekeeper* I was astonished. I should have known that being a former UN peacekeeper himself, Michael knows the drill all too well. Many of his poems are truly remarkable and it is not surprising that they have earned him awards. He knows that the task of the UN Peacekeeper is often Sisyphus-like, trying to separate warring parties and restore order, knowing that all the effort is only temporary – a sticking plaster over a wound that will be opened again by a new generation.

The Peacekeeper guards his post
Observing the past.
The same ground of ancient wars
This No-Man's Land.
He hears the whispers of remorse
From dead leaves,

Falling on secret cemeteries.
There is no end to old stories,
And he sees in the sand
The page where his part is written.

No Man's Land, Michael J. Whelan

Like most of my fellow Irish soldiers I had signed up to find adventure. We became peacekeepers by accident. Those who ended up fighting for their lives certainly found adventure – much more than they had bargained for. Large numbers of them volunteered for a second tour of duty – like the 38th Battalion – to 'finish the job' in the Congo. They did finish the job – along with the Swedes, the Ethiopians, the Italians, the Indians and the Ghanaians. It is thanks to them that my first tour of duty in the Congo was a cakewalk – and a peaceful end to the Congo campaign. I was spared the horrors of battle and I don't know if I would have had the courage and the bravery to face the danger encountered – and embraced – by young men like John Gorman who was only seventeen years old when he found himself under fire in a trench in Jadotville. The performance of A Company, 35th Battalion at Jadotville and the performance of the 36th Battalion at The Tunnel in Elizabethville left the opposing forces in the province of Katanga in no doubt that 'the fighting Irish' did not earn that title by accident! I am sure that as peacekeepers – or 'peace enforcers', the mandate bestowed on our troops for the first time in the Congo – we have played a part. It may have been a small part, but I hope that in some way, it has been significant.

My own life had been anything but peaceful. Music soothed my pain in small doses; then I returned to my shattered life, becoming more exhausted, unable to get a decent night's sleep and having to lie down several times during the day. My room, with curtains drawn at all times became my hermit's cave, shunning the light. The world outside my window became more distant – and the more distant the better. Sleep relieved the pain in my other knee, it brought escape from memories, from guilt, from anger and even from talking to friends. Sometimes, I wished I wouldn't wake up.

Each time, some force of life brought me back but with it came responsibility – an obligation – to be grateful. Gratefulness is a new skill, one that is hard to cultivate. A powerful organisation had ruined me. People had not been kind to me. What was there to be grateful for? Then, on waking, the manuscript and all that came with it would slowly penetrate the habitual thoughts and the dark intentions and give rise to the possibility that all was not lost. In J.J. R. Tolkien's book, *The Lord of the Rings* the wizard, Gandalf says,

> *Some believe it is only great power that can hold evil in check. But that is not what I have found. I found it is the small, everyday deeds of ordinary folk that keep the darkness at bay – small acts of kindness and love.*

As my story developed, I realised that it has been the deeds of those 'ordinary folk' – in the defence forces and in civilian life, deeds often overlooked – that had helped me. These are the people who, miraculously seem to be keeping the darkness at bay. In writing this story, I found myself slowly opening up and sharing the burden and in doing so it occurred to me that while many of us have suffered, maybe our suffering has brought something of value to our lives, lives that might otherwise have been bland and one dimensional. Maybe my experiences will bring something of value to others too – those whose experiences might have been similar to mine. They may never want to reveal their secrets – for many reasons – and their wishes in this regard must be respected. But it might help to let them know that they are not alone.

Not long ago I watched a television interview with a sixteen-year-old boy from County Kerry. Donal Walsh had been suffering from terminal cancer. He was given only months to live but he had out-lived the prognosis and on borrowed time, he had launched a nationwide appeal to young people who might be contemplating suicide to think again. His appeal had gone viral and he shot into the headlines. As I watched the interview I thought of the times when I had come close to killing myself and was struck by what he said about the futility of suicide. Donal had gone public to remind us all that we should value our life, every minute of it, and that we should be thankful for all the small, everyday things we take for granted. "We have limited time here and life is exquisite, even in its ordinariness," he said. The way in which Donal chose to live his final months was as powerful as his message to others. His selfless-ness during this time and the way in which he carried himself exem-plified the dignity of his acceptance of his own death while making the most of what life he had left.

I was amazed at his faith. Remembering how angry I was with God I felt rather small compared to him, a mere child. Young Donal Walsh placed himself, as he said, 'in God's hands.' I had abandoned faith in God and in life. Today, I have begun to find hope and in some existential way, continue to pray. My misfortune was to have encountered an individual within the army who preyed on my innocence. The horrendous impact that his assault had on me physically, mentally and emotionally, has defined the greater part of my life. But I have slowly begun to realise that I do have much to be thankful for. Brendan O'Connor, the host of the televi-sion programme who interviewed Donal Walsh said, "Donal's mes-sage was so true that it could sound like a cliché." It took Donal's message to penetrate my anger and my cynicism.

Sometime after I watched the programme, I met my former boss from Fermoy at the funeral of a colleague. Through my own fault, he and I had fallen out and as a result I had left Fermoy with a broken heart. When I met him again I felt compelled to go and talk to him. We shook hands. As far as I am concerned a handshake signifies the end of a dispute. As I shook his hand I felt the old gripes between us fall away. I think he was glad to see me. I was very glad to see him.

CHAPTER 11

Reflections of a Child Soldier

Because much of my adult life was spent overseas and because my mind was filled with torment, I missed a lot of what was happening at home. In March 1966 Nelson's Pillar, Dublin's iconic landmark, was blown up by the Provisional IRA and it made international news headlines. This threatened to disrupt the golden jubilee commemoration of the 1916 Easter Rising four weeks later. But the week-long ceremonies began on a warm, bright, breezy Sunday in April with a special Mass at the Pro-Cathedral, followed by a military parade past the GPO where President, Éamon de Valera, himself a veteran of the Rising, took the salute. Taoiseach, Seán Lemass was mindful that the tone of the events was essential in achieving the objectives of assuring the population at a time of economic uncertainty that there would be better things to come and to emphasise the successes and achievements of independent Ireland. I was there because I was part of the ceremonies. It was just over a year since Jerusalem and I was having a hard time. Dressed as a soldier, dying inside, I found it impossible to share in the buoyant mood of the city.

But Ireland was changing and there were better things to come. One of them was free education; educational prospects that had been denied to working class children like me were about to improve. In September, as I was preparing for another peacekeeping mission to Cyprus, Minister for Education, Donogh O'Malley announced that every child in the country could avail of free second-level education. The option of finishing school, hitherto the preserve of a minority who could afford to pay for it, would now be an opportunity for all.

Seán Lemass' economic policy took off like a rocket and transformed the country from the one that I grew up in, described as xenophobic, stagnant, dull, poor, culturally backward, and ruled from the pulpit. The changes have been rapid. From the Ireland of the 1950s and 1960s, the flow of people in the 1990s and early 2000s had changed from mass emigration to mass immigration as the so-called 'boom years' turned the country into a building site. New business parks, hotels and golf courses sprouted across the landscape and workers from Poland, Romania, Czechoslovakia and many parts of Asia followed the money and landed here. Education, while still disentangling from the grip of religion, is focused on training the young for this world of trade, investment and research and development. But changes are so rapid that in five years from now the needs of Commerce may well have taken on a completely new image, requiring a totally different type of workforce.

The face of the religious population changed too. The Church now tries to blend its doctrines with New Age and even pre-Christian philosophies, keeping a watchful eye on community-led trends. Social and economic change has swept the nation. Dublin is a cosmopolitan hub, filled with young, upwardly-mobile people working mostly in Finance and in the IT sector with giant multi-national corporations such as Google and the social media giant, Facebook. For these sedentary workers there is a gym in practically every office building and on almost every street in Dublin. After the gym, they hang out in trendy bars, nightclubs and in Indian, Italian and Chinese restaurants and at weekends they partake in outdoor pursuits – cycling, walking and hiking around the city parks or out in the surrounding hills. There are designated playgrounds where parents can bring their toddlers and sip coffee with friends as they watch the children romp on specially designed playground equipment for an hour or two each day. Cultural diversity, tolerance, open-minded attitudes, health and social care and education have advanced more than I would have ever imagined.

Divorce and the Marriage Referendum were cause for more celebration. On the other hand, revelations about endemic paedophilia in the Catholic Church, the story of the Magdalene Laundries and the infants buried in a septic tank in a home for unmarried mothers in Galway have opened old wounds for thousands of men and women throughout the country who survived these institutions. For others the revelations and the apologies and the redress have come too late. For too many of the survivors their lives have only been half lived and their invisible wounds are too deep.

I was oblivious to mental health and I was rather backward in my awareness of depression other than in the context of the defence forces. But, of course, people from all walks of life suffer from depression and anxiety – even PTSD. Although we are living longer these days, we are also more likely to encounter life experiences that will bring sadness, grief, loss and loneliness. For all our scientific and technological advances, we are still a long way from understanding ourselves and the 'machinery' of our own psychophysiology. Emotion can be the most difficult aspect of our human condition to deal with and almost impossible to express. When I was a young soldier, crying was not acceptable unless in a time of bereavement and then only if the deceased relative was a close family member – a parent or a sibling. In the event of such a loss the soldier would be repatriated and usually remained with his home battalion with no further overseas duties. If, on the other hand a soldier was physically injured his wounds were fixed up and he was back on duty as soon as he could stand up. If he had any attendant wounds of an emotional nature, they had to remain hidden.

I struggled to put the pieces of myself back together and failed; the emotion, even after all this time, is sometimes too deep and too painful for me. I have spent my life fighting on two fronts: the eternal, internal battle with myself and the external battle with the authorities. Through my inability to deal with my suffering I unknowingly succumbed to the rapist – and to the authorities.

I have allowed them to hold me in their grip. Perhaps the surge of energy that burst forth at my laptop in 2013 was in reality a message to do something to set myself free – a last, desperate cry for help? I don't know.

Sexual violence is a heinous crime – so powerful in its brutal ferocity that it is used as a weapon of war. As such, its effectiveness in inflicting everlasting damage on victims, rendering them helpless and fearful, is probably the most efficient weapon used in securing the control and submission of swathes of people – particularly children and young adults – in countries at the mercy of invaders. It is also an expression of hatred and revenge against a nation or a regime, often inflicted on innocent individuals who, simply by virtue of their nationality are vulnerable – like the Belgian baker's wife in the Congo.

Rape shatters the very core of a person. It is a most cruel and violent act from which victims may never recover. Its detrimental and far-reaching effects are not yet fully understood in medical circles. Words are inadequate to describe the full effects of such violence that is nothing short of the grossest evil. Although I have somehow finally reached a point at which I no longer wish to be defined by my brokenness, I cannot be myself because I don't know who or what my 'self' is. I had somehow come to terms with my brokenness and had more or less accepted that I would never be a whole person, but I could join my colleagues in the banter and I loved their company and I could perform my duties and be pleasant and affable – until 1980. Then Jerusalem resurfaced, and my world changed. My whole being burned. I was choking with anger and I became aggressive and belligerent. Even today, I drone on and on about the injustices that I encounter in life, unable to let go. Someone asked me recently if, in writing I had learned anything about myself, to which I said I had learned that I am a bigger asshole than I had previously thought!

It is good to see all of this now spoken about openly. I was very impressed when Prince Harry spoke to the *Daily Telegraph* newspaper about the hell he suffered after his mother, Diana, Princess of Wales was killed in a car crash in Paris. He was just a child of twelve and he explained that he had died emotionally at age twelve. He became angry and held onto the anger for twenty years. He wanted to punch someone. He took up boxing to release his aggression and eventually he went for therapy. I could relate because I too wanted to punch someone. In fact, back when I was grappling with anger I wanted to shoot someone! Prince Harry is now involved in a charity to raise awareness of mental health issues. Along with his brother, Prince William and sister-in-law Kate Middleton, the Duke and Duchess of Cambridge, Harry works with a charity that promotes mental health.

Here at home, Niall Breslin is at the forefront of the crusade for improvements in the discussion. When Niall Breslin's book, *Me and My Mate, Jeffrey* was recommended to me I was reluctant to read a book about depression. Eventually, I decided to buy the kindle version and was astonished at the title of the first chapter – 'The Holy Land'. What was the connection between a young musician and former rugby player from Mullingar in County Westmeath and the place where my nightmare had begun? Before I reached the second chapter, I realised that we had much in common – not least that I had worked with Niall's father in the army! Commandant Enda Breslin and I were staff officers in Army Headquarters in 1985. We were tasked with completing an audit of accounts of the Defence Forces' Officers Mess at McKee Barracks. Enda was President of the Audit Board. He was easy to work with – and had a good sense of humour. He had also served as an officer with the Irish UN peace-keeping force in South Lebanon in the early 1990s. It was shortly after returning from a three-month stay with his father and the rest of his family, living just a forty-five-minute drive from his father's camp in South Lebanon that Niall's troubles began.

As a twelve-year-old child, Niall had been in a war-zone, exposed indirectly to war through talk of war, to the sounds of war, to the ground tremors that shook the apartment where the family lived and to the fear that must have been palpable despite the games of football with neighbour's kids and the efforts of his parents to hold onto normality and pretend it was a holiday. As a youngster of eighteen, I was in a war-zone, but I thought the army had my back; that I was safe in the arms of an organisation that I loved. I was proud to be carrying out an important job on behalf of the government of my country, the United Nations and the people that I was sent overseas to protect, *a pilgrim of a new age*. But I had barely left home, with not a clue about life other than a childlike sense of right and wrong. When I joined the Irish Army, I had to have my parents' consent. They were required to sign my application, effectively handing me over to the care and protection of the army, a military arm of the Irish State. I was a member of the Irish Army, but I was not a casualty of war; I was the victim of a crime committed by a member of the Irish Army. The army refused to acknowledge it. The army let me down. Sadly, the army had let others down too.

In October 1986, Victor Murtagh was twenty-one years old and beginning his first tour of duty in Lebanon when he was exposed to what were described as 'a number of dangerous and stressful incidents that traumatised him'. A month later, he was unwell and was hospitalised but when discharged, he was allowed to return to duty. Shortly afterwards, two Irish soldiers were killed, one of whom was a close friend of his. In the following weeks and months, he was suffering more than most from the stressful events around him and was showing clear signs of stress including uncontrollable shaking and trembling. He was described as being a changed man when he came back to Ireland in April 1987. He was difficult and irritable and had flashbacks and difficulty sleeping. His marriage eventually broke down. But it was not until ten years later that Victor Murtagh was diagnosed with post-traumatic stress disorder. He sued the State for damages and won but the High Court decision was appealed. Then in July 2018, the Supreme Court ruled that the

State had breached its duty of care to Victor Murtagh by failing to diagnose and treat his post-traumatic stress disorder and that there was 'credible evidence' to support his. The Court laid blame with the army. It found that his commanding officers should have been alerted to the fact that he was particularly susceptible to post-traumatic stress, that there was a delay in the diagnosis and treatment of PTSD, meaning Mr Murtagh continued to suffer and deteriorate, and he was awarded damages. His solicitor said that the case would have implications for others, as it imposed an obligation and duty on the State – and in particular on the Irish Army, to look after its personnel when they are sent to war zones. He said it showed the army must look after its people and if they suffered psychological injuries, the State had a duty of care to diagnose and treat them.

I have never met Victor Murtagh; he began his first overseas mission just as I was coming to the end of my army career. But I can empathise with the twenty-one-year-old who journeyed to Lebanon, no doubt with a light heart and a hope that he would be a peacekeeper who would, in some way contribute to the cause of peace. Unlike Victor Murtagh's case, my battle with the State didn't make news headlines because it was settled out of court. Part of me regrets that I didn't appeal the settlement and I was appalled that the Supreme Court reduced the damages to Mr. Murtagh by half. But I am pleased for him and wish him well in his recovery.

Changes at this level happen all too slowly but at least changes are afoot. A rising chorus of voices, each telling its story is blending into a symphony of justified anger that has been suppressed by Church and State for generations.

CHAPTER 12

The Price of Peace

We have one of the finest peacekeeping forces in the world.
That did not happen by accident; it happened because
of the efforts of people like you.

- Mary McAleese, President of Ireland, 1997-2011
at Áras an Uachtaráin, November 2010

In a photograph, taken on an OPS post – Mount Juliet in Cyprus – shortly before the fateful trip to Jerusalem, I am sitting wearing my UN baseball cap. A friend, Gunner Patrick Lynch from Mullingar is kneeling beside me. At the time, I was aware that someone was taking photographs. There was always someone hanging around with a camera and I was feeling self-conscious and uneasy. On seeing the photograph recently, a friend observed that Patrick was looking at me intently as if he sensed my unease, something that had escaped my notice. At any rate I was reminded that coming up to my nineteenth birthday I was still a shy, introverted teenager, vulnerable and unsure of who I was; awkward in many ways. Within a few short weeks, I would suffer a shocking, grotesque awakening to the presence of evil in the world. From then on, I would adopt a fighting position – the only way I knew how to protect myself. In doing so, I remained on alert status and approached every challenge by first adopting a defensive attitude – just in case. We were trained to fight. I had spent two years up to the age of eighteen, learning to *fight*! I had done a tour of duty in the Congo and I thought I was a grown-up. But I was still a child with no understanding of relationships, of life or the ways of the world. I had not acquired any life skills through experience and I was incapable of making my own way in life. I am sure there were many like me; child soldiers. Friends plead with me to give up fighting with people, to leave grudges and anger behind. I tell them this will not happen; it's too late. I was trained as a soldier. I have a high IQ but if I were to take a psychometric test today I would probably fall down in the area on which many organisations in the corporate world place great emphasis – Emotional Intelligence.

But despite the immaturity of young soldiers in the past, Irish Military Archives are awash with acts of courage and heroism from the foundation of the State and before. We in the armed forces have given a good account of ourselves, both at home and in far-flung regions where many have had to fight for their lives and the lives of those they were there to protect. According to former Chief of Staff of the Irish defence Forces, Lieutenant-General, Seán McCann, speaking at the fiftieth anniversary commemoration of the first deployment of Irish troops on the mission to the Congo in 1960, we were the 'pathfinders', the 'pioneers' in whose footsteps present-day troops follow. Many of us were children really, but despite our ignorance and innocence, we have, according to Seán McCann, set a shining example to the Irish Defence Forces, to the United Nations, to the Irish government and to the people of Ireland.

But it has taken the heroic persistence of veterans like John Gorman to get this message through to a government minister and it has taken books – and recently a full-length feature film – to highlight another side to our history. The youngsters who had held out in the mining town of Jadotville in the Congo were exposed to injury and death. Under a barrage of mortar and machine-gun fire from a mercenary-led force several times their strength, a force augmented by a fighter jet that dropped bombs on them in their trenches, they survived – by the grace of God, their bravery and the military capabilities and the genuine concern of their commanding officer, Commandant Pat Quinlan whose primary duty was the safety of his men. If they had been repatriated in coffins they would have been heroes and martyrs. Instead, they were greeted with contempt and were deemed cowards and traitors in their homeland – even by their comrades-in-arms. The Department of Defence had little room for sentiment. The higher echelons of the army, the Irish government and the United Nations allowed this propaganda to continue for over forty years. But the spirit is unconquerable and nowhere was this more evident than among the small band of Irish soldiers, marooned at the town of Jadotville in 1961, whose spirit endured throughout their ongoing fight to have the slur of cowardice lifted. In June 2017, they were finally rewarded in a parting gesture of recognition by outgoing Taoiseach, Enda Kenny. In June 2018 the media carried the news that A Company, 35th Battalion would be awarded medals for bravery. As Declan Power, security and defence analyst whose book, *The Siege at Jadotville* led to the making of the film of the same name said, "The right result".

The youngsters who died at Niemba were the victims of poor army intelligence and inadequate local knowledge. They were left isolated in the jungle surrounded by hostile, warring tribes. When the two survivors told their stories, they were laughed at – even by those with whom they served. One of them suffered the most horrendous injuries and was left by the Baluba tribe for dead. He was nursed back to physical health by a team of Belgian doctors and nurses in a Belgian hospital in Elizabethville but when he arrived back in Ireland he was interrogated by his own Defence Forces' medics and then cast onto the scrapheap of the unemployed – with a wife and infant to support – to suffer nightmares for the rest of his life.

Two soldiers were killed in At Tiri, in Lebanon and two soldiers died at Deir Ntar, in Lebanon. At Tibnin Bridge an Irish soldier opened fire on three of his comrades. As they lay bleeding on the ground, he finished each one off with a bullet through the head. Three young men had thought that the army had their backs. A cold-blooded murderer had slipped through the cracks in the system. These soldiers have paid the ultimate price for peace. Many more returned from overseas, broken. Large numbers of those who survived conflict have never again found peace – myself included. My physical body shut down long ago, but compulsive behaviour takes over and I often respond to events – even to remarks – without due consideration or any awareness as to what others might be feeling. Sometimes my actions can give the impression that I lack respect, but I realise this only in hindsight, or after someone has pointed it out to me.

When I was raped by a fellow Irish soldier in the so-called safety and security of a small Irish group on a tour organised by, and in the care of the Irish Defence Forces, my personal development was relegated to a far-off region in my psyche and it would never to be retrieved. The event itself was bad enough. The subsequent 'trial' by a succession of civilian and army psychiatrists in order to qualify for a pension and above all, the scurrilous hypothesis that must surely be based on complete ignorance that I was making it all up, are some of the reasons that I felt compelled to write. I wanted acknowledgement for a crime that was committed against me and the subsequent denial of my right to justice.

A long time ago I reported the rapist's whereabouts to a high-ranking officer. I said that I knew he was a potential risk to youngsters but did not divulge how I knew this. My concerns were dismissed, and nothing was ever done. While the army harboured a criminal, somewhere out there a woman was – or is – married to that criminal. If they had children they are the children of a rapist, with a weakness for young boys. How many more lives have been destroyed by this man? How many others have been reduced to crumpled masses of pain and torment by this predator? And how many had he violated before attacking me in Jerusalem in 1965? If he served subsequent tours of duty overseas did he leave behind innocent victims already traumatised by war who were vulnerable and unprotected? How many other army veterans are his victims, too afraid to speak?

This callous individual has tarnished the good name of the men and women of the Irish Defence Forces. I loved the army and army life and as a soldier, my role in the Irish Army could perhaps have held many more possibilities but for one harrowing experience in Jerusalem at the start of my career. The trauma of that event created problems that were beyond my understanding. The inability to speak thwarted any hope of meaningful integration, created tendencies to attach myself to people on one hand and yet, on the other hand, to drive people away from me. It affected my ability to converse, which at times resulted in discordant narratives – as was evident in my very first attempt at writing it all down. My internal states are often a mystery – even to myself. Psychically I am tired, a man old before his time, a peacekeeper who has served in the cause of peace – and not found peace. People tell me I seldom smile, that I look sombre in photographs. I have sometimes wondered if, as poet, Michael Whelan has so adroitly observed, 'I am *chained forever to the Via Dolorosa*'.

But I am blessed to have my siblings and extended family and I am fortunate to have some true friends who kindly tolerate my idiosyncratic ways and shortcomings. I am thankful for all the small, everyday things that I used to take for granted – and I have music to provide a balsam for my soul. I am still a soldier, proud to be part of a legacy begun in 1960 that has probably affected more change than we will ever know. Today, our troops continue that legacy. When they come in contact with people whose lives have been shattered by war I am sure that in the course of their duties the majority of them demonstrate the other side – the true heart of the peacekeeper:

> *I stood there in the bowel of*
> *her existence,*
> *slack-jawed in the middle*

of that frozen room,
rifle under my arm.
It was Christmas time at home.
How do I sort this out?
No-one can threaten hunger with bullets.
Tiny hands are in my pockets.
I give her my watch.

The Family (Kosovo) – from *Peacekeeper* by Michael J. Whelan

I believe that as a nation we are very fortunate to have, as former President, Mary McAleese put it, one of the finest peacekeeping forces in the world. In her address in 2010 to the veterans of the Congo she went on to say, "This did not happen by accident; it happened because of the efforts of people like you". I am proud to be one of them – the pathfinders. Today, despite the dark secrets of the old, 'hidden army', that reputation is still intact. For a long time, beneath the gilded reputation of the Irish Defence Forces lay a dark side that was somehow missed by those tasked with screening applicants for their suitability for service. But that has changed. Thanks to new legislation, the Irish military are considered world leaders in terms of their dignity at work and their workplace equality policies. Sexual assault is recognised as a crime. Victims are treated with dignity and respect and given support to deal with its effects. The men and women of the Irish Army, the Irish Naval Service and the Irish Air Corps are a credit to all of us. For more than half a century they have been exemplary in the execution of their duties, from humanitarian aid, to the rescue of Syrian refugees in the Mediterranean, to peacekeeping in conflict zones and to rescue missions and air ambulance services at home. Pride in their country and in their culture as well as their integrity, their courage and their belief in a cause gives us all hope as they continue to serve under the flag of the United Nations and the flag of the Irish

Nation in the only cause worth serving – the cause of peace.

It has taken me over fifty years to break the silence that had become unbearable. This is a story that I could never bring myself to tell, a painful and disturbing journey back in time that opened up a deep wound. For all of that time I believed that like Frodo in *The Lord of the Rings*, and the king. Amfortas in *Parsifal*, I had a wound that would not heal – that would never heal.

I stumbled into the world of writing. Like Parsifal who was trying to kill a swan, I was trying to 'kill' those who had cheated me. The pensions debacle had caused secondary PTSD and, as I can now see, it ruined my health because I could not let it go. It consumed my mind, night and day. My world was an ever-shrinking and miserable place and I didn't know what else to do, which frustrated me even more. I fell ill and was hospitalised, many times, the time between admissions becoming shorter and shorter.

Finally allowing myself to speak, albeit it falteringly at first resulted in a minor miracle: when I did speak I was heard, without judgement – and understood. I don't wish to discount the years of therapy, as some of the therapy helped in many ways. When I look back, I realise that every experience provided some insight. But this book has been the most cathartic and revealing – and an unexpected challenge. I cannot forget Jerusalem but little by little, the straitjacket is beginning to loosen and at the very least, I can speak about the past from a stronger place inside. I may never be able to love – even like – myself but while I still have a soft spot for *The Myth of Sisyphus,* the evidence for meaning and a higher perspective is slowly mounting. Incidents of depersonalisation seem to be a lot less frequent. Yoga breathing, learned late in life, as well as sheer force of will helped me through a very dodgy episode of a cardiac nature during a recent stay in Vienna. A visit to my cardiologist on my return home resulted in a change of medication. In March 2018, I had to have a second Cather ablation. For now, things have settled down again.

But I am still angry, and I am still plagued by physical problems. But I ask for God's forgiveness for the perpetrator of the crime and I wish him peace. I ask for forgiveness for myself for having carried the burden for over fifty years. I don't yet know what inner peace feels like. But to be content, like the youth of nineteen, the Two Star private with a UN medal… that would be enough.

JERUSALEM

Who is the man I see
where I'm supposed to be?
I was the pilgrim of a new age,
a soldier cast in the church of my homeland,
the Peacekeeper come to the gates of the City of David,
where my heart, broken, stumbled
on the salt rocks of a desert.

In that cauldron of the Holy Lands
I was shaded by the memory of the Cedar,
I walked in the Passion of Christ,
my innocence might have changed the world
but that Calvary is my Golgotha.
Unlike Barabbas I am chained forever
to the *Via Dolorosa*.

Many times I have witnessed the caravans
leave the City of Heaven
and I longed to go home, un-scourged.
There are no palms for my feet to walk upon
in the souks and the aromas of this city
and in the places where I pray.
I am not the man I was meant to be.
My soul was taken by a beast I try to forgive,
who left me in this hell where I continue to writhe.
This is my testament to the walls of Jerusalem -
I was nineteen when the Hosannas ended!

Michael J. Whelan
September 2016

Acknowledgements

My sincere thanks to Declan Power for reading this story and writing the Foreword. This is a great honour as Declan is well-respected as a security and defence analyst who has worked throughout Africa and the Middle East. He was a career soldier who served in the three combat arms of the Irish Army, attended the Military College and served within the higher echelons of Defence Headquarters. He is the author of the book *Siege at Jadotville*: the Irish Army's Forgotten Battle which has been adapted for film and broadcast by Netflix in 2016. I would like to take this opportunity to offer my congratulations to Declan on his success.

To my friend, Michael Whelan, MA for his poem, *Jerusalem* which he wrote specifically for this story and for permission to use his poems, *No Man's Land*, and *Grapes of Wrath* from his collection of poetry, 'Peacekeeper', published by Daoire Press, 2016, sincere and heartfelt thanks.

This book could not have been written without my 'ghost', Imelda Conway Duffy. Her hard work and dedication were inspirational and her good humour lifted me at times when the burden of the story was overwhelming, and I was in a dark place. Thank you, Imelda.

To the wonderful sisters Áine and Cáit Skelly at The Rathcoole Business Centre, Rathcoole, Co. Dublin I owe a debt of gratitude.

Review Requested:
If you loved this book, would you please provide a review at
Amazon.com?

Lightning Source UK Ltd.
Milton Keynes UK
UKHW011814100519
342490UK00003B/13/P